For

This was my dissertation for the Mass
Psychology, written as part of my doct
well and didn't get so bogged down in
pscyhobabble style that it could stand a   ⌐ ⌐ɪ ɪɪon-
fiction, or literate cultural criticism.

Why write if not readable?

The acknowledgements and dedications still stand as fresh as the day the
first copy was printed.

Enjoy, and if Nikki Sixx is out there reading this and wants to do an album
with me...

Seth A. Doolin
Salem, Massachusetts
May 2009

WE MAY LOOK LIKE CHICKS BUT WE CAN STILL KICK YOUR ASS:

METAL GLAM AS A REFLECTION OF MASCULINITY IN TRANSITION

SETH A. DOOLIN, Psy.D.

Abstract

Masculinity as a social construction in transition is examined using Metal Glam of the 1980s as a benchmark. Metal Glam, as popular culture, will be shown to be a reflection of the larger culture's anxieties and concerns about gender and gender differentiation within an historical and cultural context. The social and cultural history of the concept and definition of masculinity will be examined, and the popular culture movements of Rock and Roll, Heavy Metal, British Glam, will be put into this social and historical context to demonstrate Metal Glam as representative of a culture's grappling with the elusive concept of gender and gender roles. The psychological historical backdrop, particularly masculine/feminine scales, androgyny, gender identity development, and gender theory will also be addressed as a contributing factor.

DEDICATION

This study is dedicated to my father and future sons.

ACKNOWLEDGEMENTS

As with any project, there are a great many people to be thanked. First and foremost is my fiancée Kelly Barrington, who not only provided emotional and intellectual (not to mention caffinated) support, but also demonstrated patience and tolerance around the research of this project. Such research included the listening of Heavy Metal for days on end, giggling to myself while reading and writing, tolerating my writer's block tantrums, and buying me an electric guitar for Christmas in order to help me get more involved in the subject matter I was studying.

Secondly, I thank my committee, all three of whom have been intellectual mentors for me during my time at MSPP. Jill Bloom's intellectual stamp of deconstructing tropes of gender can certainly be seen as a direct influence here. Bob Jampel's careful scholarship (i.e., calling me on it when I was trying to pile it on) deserves much thanks. And Sam Moncata's guidance, encouragement, and synthetic integration of person and context are also owed a debt in this work.

I wish to thank my support group, nicknamed "the Testicles" and their wives: David Ortega and Kelly Gunderson; KC Chiappa and Mandy Cross; and Mark Simmons and Amy Galatis. Our support group really didn't meet that often, and we weren't really all that supportive in actual practice, but as Spinal Tap suggests of their message of brotherly love, the intent of support was very clear among the four of us. After the first semester, we were the only four men in our year of the program. Over time we forged a supportive relationship which included joint projects such as the "Dora, Dora, Dora" film, and a number of follies sketches. Although we only met twice during the actual writing of the dissertation, their support was felt in other ways.

I also thank Beth Svajian, whose previous scholarship got me started and whose collection of books kept me going.

Other acknowledgements I wish to make at this time are to Fran Mervyn, for accepting me into the program; Brian Ott for his personal and theatrical support; Alan Beck and Stan Berman for their support and guidance for the first two years of the program; Norby Mintz for his support and gentle nagging throughout the entire four years of this program; Ed DeVos for not flunking me in statistics; past and present supervisors Nancy Moczynski, Skip Reilly, Bob Caggiano and Barry Skoff, each of whom have left their stamp on my clinical work; Kari Mitchell Flynn for her unflagging support, humor, and assistance; and finally, I should thank Nick Covino for his good nature, sense of humor, and most importantly, for tolerating me during the past year.

This dissertation was made possible by a grant from the Mary and Joseph Doolin foundation, without whose generosity, support, and charity, my graduate education would not be possible.

Seth A. Doolin
Boston
April 11, 2003

PREFACE

I find it interesting that I am putting the finishing touches on my dissertation on April 11, 2003. Dates and numbers and their significance have always held a fascination for me, and the completion of my thesis on April 11 is no exception as this is the date of Anton Szanzor LaVey's birthday (1930-1997). This is coincidental not only because LaVey was the founder of the Church of Satan, and befriended Marilyn Manson, but this thereby links Metal Glam's past and present in the darkness exuded by Black Sabbath, the fact that Niiki Sixx's read LaVey's *Satanic Bible* while writing *Shout at the Devil*, and the reading of Manson as a fusion of anarchist, antichrist and androgyne.

The real significance of finishing my dissertation on LaVey's birthday, though, is when you get past all that theatrical "dark side" imagery, when you put aside LaVey's Albert Ellis/Libertarian musings, moving past the pulpy platitudes and getting to an often overlooked aspect of LaVey's "philosophy": that which is forbidden is fun.

That's really what Rock and Roll is all about: doing the forbidden and finding it fun. Rock and Roll started out as a progression from American Blues, basically is was music by and for Black audiences that White audiences appropriated, mostly because of the strictly drawn racial lines of the times. Rock and Roll was dangerous and daring in the 1950s due to its link to Black culture. That's part of what made it fun. I'll bet part of my father's fascination with Chuck Berry and Fats Domino was that his father hated them, and their being Black probably had something to do with it.

As times change the forbidden and the shocking also change. In the 1960s drugs and free love were taboos to be broken: the Byrds' *Eight Miles High*, tame by our standards today was quite controversial. After sex was no longer shocking, playing with gender *was* shocking. David Bowie and Marc Bolan's T.Rex raised eyebrows and parental concerns in the UK as the New York Dolls stirred controversy in America.

Rock and Roll is built on rebellion, dabbling in the forbidden, whether that forbidden is sex, drugs, androgyny, misogyny, the occult, gender bending, gender straightening, unraveling gender straightjackets, or putting on straightjackets and downing thorazine. Whatever you're not supposed to do or be Rock and Roll touts as the Next Big Thing.

8

Groucho said "Whatever it is, I'm against it"; the Ramones just said "I'm against it"; and Twisted Sister said "We're not gonna take it". The roots of Rock and Roll are rebellion, refusal, and the fun of the forbidden. Heavy Metal, British Glam, and Metal Glam all reveled in the forbidden and had fun with it. Behind the dour and bleak lyrics of Black Sabbath was the sheer enjoyment of embracing taboos. The British Glam scene wore its humor loudly and brightly, and Metal Glam was all about the hedonistic enjoyment and giddy abandon in the role of the outlaw, the outsider, the heretic.

In terms of my experience with this project, I, too, was engaging in something somewhat forbidden and having fun with it. The very idea of one's doctoral project focusing on not only Rock and Roll, not only Heavy Metal, but Metal Glam was something on the outer edge of accepted psychology. People outside of MSPP are always a little taken aback when I tell them what I've been working on for the past year and a half. I think this also gave me the conviction to continue my work on this project: to break down the conventional barriers of what is psychology and what is not psychology. I find psychology often limits itself in its areas of inquiry and this only further marginalizes us as a field, as a discipline.

Aside from my own rebellious leanings in psychology, I also worked on this for a year and a half because it was fun (maybe part of the fun was the eyebrows I would raise when I described my study). I would listen to Heavy Metal for hours on end, thoroughly enjoying myself, but also immersed in research. I would read Mötley Crüe's collective autobiography and laugh out loud, Kelly would come in from the next room and make some comment about how diligently I was working. Everything I did was somehow tied up in this project: I would play my guitar, and in the riffs I would reflect on the musical foundation of Heavy Metal and how the structure of the guitar contributed to the sound and feel of Heavy Metal; I would watch the Simpsons and Seinfeld reruns and reflect on the constructions of masculinity portrayed in the medium of television; or I would browse book stores and note the separate sections for Women's Studies, yet no sections for Men's Studies, and think about the implicit message in our culture that masculinity is rarely discussed openly but transmitted silently and indirectly. While Feminism has official texts and bodies of literature, masculinity only has lowbrow exploitive television such as Comedy Central's "The Man Show" and the short-lived FX network's "X-Show".

But I digress.

9

The bottom line here is the fact that I had fun writing this.
I can only hope that it is fun for people to read.
As well as psychologically sound and relevant.
Seth A. Doolin
Boston, April 11, 2003

Table of Contents

Introduction: "*We May Look Like Chicks, But We Can Kick Your Ass!*[i]"

"We may look like chicks, but we can kick your ass!" (Mötley Crüe, 1986). This sentiment has been uttered by members of Mötley Crüe, Poison, Faster Pussycat, Cinderella, LA Guns, Britny Fox, and perhaps countless other mascaraed musicians during the mid 1980s (Mötley Crüe, 1986; Spheeris, 1988; Debonne & Santiago, 2000). This was the age of big hair, spandex, lipstick, foundation, eyeshadow, eyeliner, mascara, high-heeled boots, mesh tops, and brightly colored tight pants, worn by the male performers. This was the age of the preening and pouting androgynously adorned rock and roller who was equal parts attitude and Aqua Net. This was the age of Metal Glam.

The central problem addressed by this study will be making sense of the androgynous presentation in Metal Glam of the 1980s, especially in context of preadolescent male gender identity development. The context of the adolescent is then placed within the larger context of the 1980s as being an historic point in time in which various cultural forces contribute to construct masculinity. This construct of masculinity is dealt with not only as a concept informed by culture and informing culture, but also as an experience, an identity, a crisis in "being" as America moves from a Preindustrialized cultural organization to a Postwar cultural organization. Part of this cultural organization is the organization of experience as gendered.

Unpacking the Puzzle of Metal Glam

In Metal Glam, hypermasculinity is combined with stylistic elements of the feminine, posing the question of how one makes sense of this seeming clash of elements. Within the theatrical and androgynous presentation of the Metal Glam icon are combined elements of individual gender identity development, cultural notions of gender role, the cultural history of patriarchy and masculinity, youth culture, and cultural representation. Additionally, the cultural representation aspect of stylistic iconography in popular culture necessarily lends itself to analysis at the level of symbolism and semiotics. It will be the work of this study to tease out the historic and cultural determinants of Metal Glam, positioning this genre of rock and roll as emblematic of a culture in transition with regard to gender identity development, particularly, the notion of masculinity in

17

transition from a "traditional" masculinity to a "more inclusive" form of masculninity.

What makes the cultural and historical phenomenon of Metal Glam interesting to an exploration of masculinity in transition is that while the Metal Glam performers presented an image of transgressive gender bending and androgyny in the appropriation of stylized aspects of the feminine, their lyrical content and manner were hypermasculine to the point of misogyny, as will be demonstrated shortly.. In fact, the image and presentation of the Metal Glam icon may be read as misogyny masking or *vamping* as androgyny. The androgynous icon of Metal Glam becomes a clash in elements of gender performativity, a visual and textual battleground between glossy lipstick and testosterone fueled primal sexuality. Within this clash of stylized and socially constructed sex roles is embodied the clashes and tensions within the concept and construction of masculinity itself during the 1980s. Before further exploring the social and cultural implications of Maxx Factor and Marshall stacks[ii], closer attention needs to be paid to the clash of elements within the androgynous icon of Metal Glam.

Jump In The Fire[iii]: Method, Sources, Scope, and Relevance

1. Method

As a thorough exploration of the Metal Glam genre would be exhaustive, exhausting, and beyond the scope of this study, the performers and bands cited in this study have been selected as a representative sample of the genre. I shall draw on examples primarily from Mötley Crüe, Poison, Faster Pussycat, Cinderella, Britny Fox, LA Guns, and Guns N Roses and these bands have a high degree of agreement as representative of the genre of Metal Glam among critics and authors on heavy metal culture (Klosterman, 2002a; Konow, 2002; Walser 1993; Weinstein, 2000). Also, these bands represent the beginning and end points of the chronology of Metal Glam, so we may actually look at Metal Glam's evolution over time and place this within the larger historical framework in addition to viewing Metal Glam as a frozen moment in time that reflects upon the larger culture.

The primary unit of analysis will be the album, including the elements of the cover art, the lyrical content within, as well as the musical style of the album's sound, not unlike the manner in which Roland Barthes or Umberto Eco dissect the style of genre via language in literature in their

18

field of semiotics. Occasionally archival interview material from filmed documentaries may be used to illustrate a point, however, as the album was the primary unit of consumption in the 1980s (as opposed to the single of the 1950s or 1960s, or the MP3 file at present), most of the source material for Metal Glam will be taken from the albums themselves.

At present, there is virtually nothing in the psychological literature that speaks directly to the problem of male preadolescent gender identity development related to Metal Glam of the 1980s. The psychological literature provides a wealth of information on the concept of gender role and gender identity development, as well as some information on psychological androgyny and the concept of self, creativity, and interpersonal functioning. Some of the psychological literature casts a wider net onto the concept of social and cultural construction of gender identity, and some of the literature addresses the construct of masculinity in transition. However, the psychological literature has little directly to say about the widespread cultural phenomenon of Metal Glam, which was not only a dominant presence in popular culture during the 1980s, and has continued to be a readily recognizable historical icon. The fact that Metal Glam appealed to a predominantly preadolescent audience, at a stage in which individual and gender identity developmental issues are assumed to be prevalent, and given that this cultural genre traded as heavily in gender representation should have been of greater interest to psychology. Where the cultural and historical phenomenon of Metal Glam can be of interest to psychology is as a window into understanding something about male preadolescent gender identity at a particular point in time, which may also tell us something about the history of masculinity in American culture. Specifically, Metal Glam may tell us something about masculinity in transition during the 1980s.

As the vast literature of Psychology is relatively silent on the subject of Metal Glam and the significance of androgyny in Rock and Roll, we instead piece together a psychological understanding of our central problem from the fragments of its many aspects: we can find literature on the measurement of and conceptualization of masculinity and femininity; we can find literature on adolescent development (given the target audience of Rock and Roll in general); we can find literature on the construction of a self, even a gendered self; and we can find literature on gender presentation. This literature is reviewed as the fragmentary aspects of our central problem are touched upon, preparing the way for a synthesis in the final chapter.

19

2. Significance

Despite the fact that the 1980s have passed, and Metal Glam is no longer at the forefront of popular culture, a brief perusal of the current media attests to a cultural fascination with the 1980s. Documentaries on "hair bands" on VH1, the reunion tour of Poison, new albums by Poison and Motley Crue, books featured in the New York Times Book Review, and record company re-issues of 1980s metal and Metal Glam all attest to a fascination with the 1980s as part of our postmodernist culture of recycling the past and recombining it for present commodification. Additionally, both music and cultural critic can recognize the influence of 1980s Metal Glam on present music and cultural representation. Further, we can use the cultural and historical phenomenon of Metal Glam as a benchmark in examining both gender identity and masculinity in transition. Essentially, Metal Glam may be seen as exemplifying a moment in history that illustrates the "crisis" in masculinity: the result of shifting gender roles and gender identification from a previous construction of masculinity to the next. This crisis of masculinity is played out in a reciprocal relationship between popular culture, the larger cultural and social forces, and the individual.

We will see that there has always been a crisis in masculinity, that there has always been a cultural anxiety that boyhood is threatened, either by present mothers, absent fathers, working fathers, unemployed fathers, employed mothers, war, or peace.

3. Scope

This project examines the phenomenon of Metal Glam of the 1980s through the lenses of gender theory, developmental theory, social and cultural history, and social representation. The thrust of the project is to examine the interplay between individual, development, culture, and cultural representation as these various elements combine in the image or style of Metal Glam.

Take Me Back to Paradise City Where the Grass is Green and the Girls Are Pretty[iv]: A Map of the Terrain

This study is comprised of five major chapters. The first chapter frames the question the object of inquiry. It is a formal statement of the problem under consideration: making sense of the clash in elements in the presentation of the Metal Glam androgyne. The presentation of the clash in elements present in the Metal Glam genre will also be contextualized in terms of the demographics of the audience: White, lower to upper middle class, male, in the 13 to 19 year old range (this too will become more specific). The "gendering" of Heavy Metal and subsequently Metal Glam will also be briefly explored.

The second chapter defines Metal Glam: what constitutes Metal Glam, and where Metal Glam is located in history. The musical genre of Metal Glam is stringently defined as to the elements of the genre, including the semiotics of style, sound, and lyrical content. Also delineated here will be the historical era under consideration. The parameters of the era will become more specific as Metal Glam will be located in history as defined by the emergence of the Metal Glam as a formal style, as documented by the release of albums noted for constituting the style of Metal Glam. The critical literature on rock and roll is utilized as source material: print material (books, music press and criticism) as well as liner notes in compact discs, and documentaries on rock and roll, especially those which include interviews with Metal Glam artists.

In this chapter, it is important to locate Metal Glam in history, not just in its prime, but to trace its antecedents which move in two converging directions. First, the history of Heavy Metal is traced to its formal roots in Black Sabbath and the resulting New Wave of British Heavy Metal (shortened as NWOBHM, often cited as inspiration by Metal Glam artists). The exploration of Heavy Metal also looks at the foundations of Heavy Metal, the proto-Metal of blues inspired rock and roll, psychedelia, and biker culture, which positions Altamont as the historical turning point for Heavy Metal and its culture.

As Metal Glam is critically understood as a hybrid of Heavy Metal and British Glam, the history of British Glam is also briefly examined, tracing these roots back to David Bowie, Marc Bolan's T-Rex, Gary Glitter, Roxy Music, and what is often referred to by critics as the "mascara revolution" of the early 1970s.

Chapter Three locates masculinity as a social construct in the 1980s. This is an era in which cultural critics, historians, social scientists, and gender theorists suggest a "crisis in masculinity". In order to describe and discuss what constitutes this "crisis", the social construction of masculinity must be examined. The work of cultural historians Michael Kimmel, Anthony Rotundo, and David Savran help to illustrate the social and cultural history of masculinity and manhood in American civilization, as well as its transitions following economic, cultural, and industrial

transformations which undergird the social construction of masculinity itself, according to these authors. Chapter three traces the historic construction of masculinity in American culture to bring the reader through the 1980s, where the work of Susan Faludi, among other cultural critics, is referred to in order to highlight and illustrate the crisis in masculinity.

Chapter three also presents the broader backdrop of popular culture in the 1980s, including Ronald Regan's "cowboy" presentation, Sam Malone's aging lotario character on the long-running sitcom Cheers, Stallone's Rambo, demographic statistics of the American family highlighting an increasing absence in the role of the father in the home, as well as examples from children's television, such as the cartoon He-Man, Master of the Universe, not to mention the rise in Professional Wrestling.

Chapter Four then places the psychological concepts of androgyny, gender identity development, and gender performativity within historical context, demonstrating the waves of scientific thought that were generating concurrently with social and cultural as well as popular cultural developments. The works of Constantinople and Bem are reviewed, as they set the stage for a socially constructed gender identity that is not necessarily tied to biological sex. Also, models of development that include gender identity are briefly reviewed, including such developmental theorists as Blos, Kegan, and Kohlberg, as well as dynamic models of gender identity development. This serves to address the intersection of the individual in development (adolescence) with social-cultural history, as well as popular culture. Finally, gender theory is introduced. Gender theory will be placed last in the list reflecting the historic chronology a growing out of a postmodern cultural ethos.

As Chapter One sets the stage, Chapters Two through Four each tell stories that run parallel to one another. These stories are presently separately for the sake of clarity, but it should not be assumed that popular music, social history, and psychology are orthogonal and purely linear. Chapter Five will pull all three histories together, tying together the pieces of Heavy Metal and British Glam's intertwining history as it intersects with social and cultural transitions in masculinity that then intersect with the audience: adolescence in transition. In addition to tracing the lines of connection from one historic phenomenon to another, Chapter Five will also examine the decline and disappearance in Metal Glam concurrent with transformations in social cultural history. Specifically, we will examine Klosterman's offhand observation that Kurt Cobain's appearance on

22

MTV's Headbanger's Ball wearing a dress signaled the death-knell to Metal Glam.

The necessary question of what this means to us in the here and now is addressed in the concluding remarks, which illustrate Metal Glam as a reflection of a culture in transition and highlight more recent developments in Rock and Roll and their significance for a culture still in transition in the construction of masculinity.

Finally, the appendix, or as it is referred to here, the *Coda*, addresses aspects of the work that while legitimate points to be raised, cannot be fully entertained due to the necessarily limited length, scope, and focus of the present work.

"We Never Say 'Love Your Brother', But the Message Should Be Clear"[v]: Limitations of The Study

Before proceeding into the history and the literature, it should be acknowledged that the primary subject group under consideration in this study is American, White, Middle Class, Suburban Males, and as noted above, the age range is primarily preadolescent to adolescent. This was largely the target audience of Metal Glam in the 1980s, as a key record-buying demographic (Walser, 1993). In other words, the packaging, image, lyrical content, videos, and concert promotion in the Heavy Metal genre in the 1980s was geared toward the White, Suburban, Middle Class preadolescent to adolescent market (Walser, 1993; Weinstein, 2000; Kloseterman, 2002a; Konow, 2003). As will be revealed in Chapter Three, the social and historical context of masculinity, this was also an age group that was considered to be vulnerable in terms of masculinity. In other words, it was at the preadolescent to adolescent stage that many Boys clubs and social supports for boys, aiming to socialize these boys into men, focused their attention (Blankenhorn, 1995; Griswold, 1993; Mintz, 1998; Rotundo, 1993). The suburban element is not a strictly biding demographic, although Savran's (1998) observation that the shift to the suburbs from urban centers served to de-center masculinity in the immediate post-World War II period. As White families moved from the cities to suburbs (casually referred to as *White flight*), Heavy Metal moved along as well. Urban centers instead became the locale for Punk, Rap, Hip-Hop, and Reggae, as well as varieties of "World Music" as the racial and

23

this is where is also shown, richly, Van Halen come from and ethnic constitutions of cities changed with successive waves of immigration.

Finally, the American aspect of our target group will become clear in Chapter Five, although it should be sufficient to mention here that the North American culture as constructed by history, economy, technology, time and place in the world are significant in the particular construction of gender and gender roles. In other words, there is something particular about American culture that contributes to how come to conceive of what it means to be masculine and what it means to be feminine, and further there is something particularly American about the emphasis we give these constructs. The simple fact that this is even a topic of investigation is also something particular to American culture.

Therefore, in terms of the generalizeability of this study, the "normative" group of American White Middle Class Suburban preadolescent to adolescent males, should be held in mind. Although Walser (1993) and Weinstein (2000) make note of African American, Latin American, and Asian American males as well as females, of various social classes, who are identified as aficionados of Heavy Metal, these are indeed outliers and the core audience of Heavy Metal remains our subject group under consideration. Before closing this chapter, it should be noted that just as the White Suburban Middle Class Male is considered the normative sample for Heavy Metal, and by extension popular culture in the 1980s, it is the same for the discipline of psychology, that until the Feminist Psychology movement, the White Middle Class male was considered to be the normative group, the representative for humanity, so far as psychology was concerned.

A Few Words About A Few Words: Stylistics

The casual reader will note that terms for musical genres have been capitalized. Terms such as Rock and Roll, Heavy Metal, Metal Glam, British Glam, Punk, Industrial, Goth, Speedmetal, and Death Metal have been intentionally capitalized in order to recognize the formality of each genre. Genres in Rock and Roll are akin to movements in Art History: some are self-identified in their own time and some are identified by others after the fact. Some bands, like Black Sabbath or Led Zeppelin, emerged before there was a genre to identify them, yet wind up defining a genre. Some bands vie for inclusion into a genre, such as Kiss, who occasionally identify themselves as Heavy Metal despite their pop stylings, or Def

24

Leppard, who distance themselves from the term Heavy Metal. Other bands, such as Metallica, Slayer, and Anthrax, consciously formed the genre of Speedmetal or Thrash and were very aware of their working definitions of the genre. The point is that genre in Rock and Roll represents an identification of both band and fans. Some bands are located on the cusp of genres, such as the Melvins, who however between Grunge and Heavy Metal, and some bands move from one genre to another, such as Suicidal Tendencies, whose first album was Hardcore Punk and second album Speedmetal[vi]. However, these genres are analogous to Psychological "camps" or schools of thought, which locate the clinician on certain theoretical grounds and world-views. As identifiable genres with defined and differentiated sounds and styles, capitalization has been employed to emphasize this differentiation.

Further, the term Metal Glam is used throughout this study, although it will be recognized that this is not the only term for the genre. Walser (1993) and Weinstein (2000) refer to Metal Glam as "lite metal", "glam metal" or alternately "poseur rock" or "poodle metal" as derogatory terms within the genre of Heavy Metal itself. The conscious choice of *Metal Glam* as a descriptive term here denotes Metal Glam as a *sub*genre of Heavy Metal, secondarily identified by its stylistic referents to British Glam. Although as Chapter Two will trace the intertwining paths of Heavy Metal and British Glam, the term *Glam Metal* would have been equally appropriate. For the sake of consistency, *Metal Glam* has been selected.

important link.
to
hyperreality

Chapter I: Formal Statement of the Problem

Dressed to Kill[vii]: The "Look" of Metal Glam

In terms of illustrating the clash in elements, the juxtaposition of stereotypic elements of the feminine combined with hypermasculinity, we will turn first to Mötley Crüe's 1983 *Shout At The Devil* (Mötley Crüe, 1983) album, frequently cited as the first official album of Metal Glam (Klosterman, 2002a, Walser, 1993, Weinstein, 2000; see Appendix 2). On the cover, each band member's hair is coifed and teased, and in addition to the "war paint" effect of streaks of black under the eyes of Nikki Sixx (upper left) or on the right upper cheek of Mick Mars and Tommy Lee (lower left and right, respectively), each member is wearing foundation and generous amounts of lipstick. Eye shadow and mascara is evident on Vince Neil (upper right), as well as on Mars and Lee.

This "look" for the band continues into their 1985 *Theatre of Pain* (Mötley Crüe, 1985) album, although it should be noted that the leather, studs, and torn mesh outfits of the *Shout at the Devil* era have been traded in for silk, sequins, scarves, and lace (see Appendix 2). By 1987's *Girls, Girls, Girls* (Mötley Crüe, 1987) (see Appendix 2), lace had been swapped for leather and motorcycles, although the teased hair and eyeliner had remained the same. In fact, even at 1989's *Dr. Feelgood* (Mötley Crüe, 1989), a time at which Mötley Crüe had openly eschewed the glam aesthetic (Strauss, 2002; Debonne & Santiago, 2000), one can still note the smooth face, glossy lips, and haunting eyes of Vince Neil on the back cover (see Appendix 2). From *Shout at the Devil* through *Dr. Feelgood*, the stylistic application of make-up and coifed hair presents these male musicians in attire and attributes traditionally associated with women, giving their appearance a feminized look, the end result being an androgynous presentation.

Motely Crue may have been at the forefront of a new genre of Metal Glam in the early 1980s, but it is important to remember that Metal Glam constituted a genre with its own sound, look, and themes which would identify Metal Glam as a genre, which will be more thoroughly discussed in the following chapter. For the present, the stylistic look of other Metal Glam artists will need to be represented.

As Mötley Crüe is credited as the innovators and progenitors of the Metal Glam style, Poison is credited with fully embodying Metal Glam. Klosterman credits Poison with perfecting the genre of Metal Glam and further describes the band as the "Glammiest of the Glammy"

26

(Klosterman, 2002a, p. 67). The cover of Poison's 1986 debut album, *Look What the Cat Dragged In* (Poison, 1986), features four close headshots, the prominent feature of the photos being the hair and make-up (see Appendix 2). In fact, the focus on hair and cosmetics and lack of referents to rock and roll (i.e., no identifying signs or symbols of rock and roll such as guitars or amplifiers) on the cover and back present the stylistic element of Metal Glam as primary for Poison, reinforcing Klosterman's above observations. *Lack of music semiotic.*

Poison's 1988 follow-up album, *Open up and Say...Ahh!* (Poison, 1988), continues glossy and stylized band member photos on the back cover (see Appendix 2), with attention to hair and make-up. What is interesting here is that the inner sleeve photos of band members present a mix of close shots that resemble modeling portfolios interspersed with photos of band members engaged in pursuits more traditionally associated with masculinity, such as skateboarding, on motorcycles, driving sports cars, or flanked by bikini-clad women. The fact that these images were dated 1988 will be demonstrated as significant in the following chapter which outlines the history of Metal Glam.

By Poison's 1990 *Flesh & Blood* album (Poison, 1990), the previous signifiers of androgyny, namely make-up, coifed hair, and highly stylized clothes had been exchanged for ripped jeans, shaggier hair, and tattoos. The cover featured the band's logo as a fresh tattoo on an anonymous arm (see Appendix 2), and the back cover photo of the band does not immediately identify their style as Metal Glam, and in fact appears indistinguishable from more mainstream rock and roll. Prior to *Flesh & Blood*, Poison's attention to hair, make-up, and highly stylized clothing, akin to the presentation of Mötley Crüe, gave them a feminized appearance, and again the end result was an androgynous presentation.

Other examples from the middle 1980s, when the Metal Glam style became a trend in popular music (Handleman & Pond, 1987; Hoskyns, 1998; Klosterman, 2002; Walser, 1993; Weinstein, 2000) may be seen in Cinderella and Britny Fox (see Appendix 2). The names of these bands should be noted for their associations to femininity. Additionally, although an overly feminized appearance is "avoided" in the lack of make-up worn by these bands, their highly stylized hair and elaborate wardrobe consisting of lace, sequins, and animal print spandex are enough associated with feminine attire to present the bands as androgynous.

Even toward the end of the 1980s, when Metal Glam became more leather than lace, and more tattoos and torn t-shirts than eyeliner and foundation, androgyny may be noted in the back cover photo for Faster Pussycat's 1987 self-titled debut (see Appendix 2) in accentuation of the eyes and lips of the band members, suggesting make-up. The same may be noted in the Guns N Roses collage on their 1987 debut *Appetite for Destruction* (see Appendix 2) where Axl Rose, behind the sunglasses appears to be made up, and his hair artfully arranged in another shot. This more "masculinized" version of androgyny may also be seen in LA Guns' self-titled 1988 debut, where despite the rugged masculinity of five male rock and rollers, some sans shirts, some tattooed, some posing with machine guns, the band is still formed around guitarist Tracii Guns, with bassist Kelly Nickels, names that have been traditionally women's names. Additionally, eye make-up is suggested on the back cover photo for their follow-up album, 1989's *Cocked and Loaded* (Appendix 2).

In summation, the stylistic presentation of Metal Glam may be described as visually *noisy*, flamboyant, and incorporating stereotypic stylistic features of the feminine, especially with regard to cosmetics and coiffure. This only becomes interesting when taken in context with the hypermasculinity of Metal Glam, which then frames the genre as represented by a clash of elements of masculine and feminine.

Given the context of rock and roll as a highly sexualized art form, from Elvis' censored pelvis, the changed line from the Rolling Stones' "Satisfaction" and *"Let's Spend the Night Together"* on the Ed Sullivan show[viii] (Deane, 1995), and Jim Morrison's rumored public exposure in Connecticut (Deane, 1995, Hopkins & Sugerman, 1995). Further censoring within the recording itself is noted in the Rolling Stones' song "Star Star" from 1973's *Goat's Head Soup* (Rolling Stones, 1973)[ix], and further pressure from political and special interested groups for the recording industry to self-censor can be seen in Tipper Gore's Parents' Music Resource Center in the mid 1980s. Given this background, it should not be surprising that much of the lyrical content of Heavy Metal in general and Metal Glam in particular should also be highly sexualized. Metal Glam, however, perhaps as a genre of Heavy Metal, perhaps as a product of the highly sexualized cultural and social climate of pre-AIDS 1980s, pushed the envelope from sexuality into the border regions of misogyny is demonstrated by the following lyrics.

From Mötley Crüe's *Shout at the Devil*, an excerpt from "Ten Seconds to Love":

Touch my gun but don't pull the trigger

Hypercalis

28

Let's make history in the elevator
Or lock the door shine my pistol some more
Here I cum just ten seconds more...

Ten seconds to love
Ten seconds to love
Just wait honey
Till I tell the boys about you
(Sixx & Neil, 1983)

The phallocentrism and merging themes of sex and agression hardly need to be highlighted here. The band's 2001 collective memoir, *The Dirt: Confessions of the World's Most Notorious Rock Band* (Strauss, 2002), contains a number of graphic and explicit narratives from the band's history that give first-hand accounts of sexually explicit and misogynistic behavior that flirt with legality.

A sampling from the Mötley Crüe's 1989 *Dr. Feelgood* album suggests objectification and misogyny as embedded in Mötley Crüe's rock and roll ethos. An excerpt from "Slice of Your Pie":

Tattoo crawling up her leg so sexy
So young...ever get caught they'll arrest me
School girl, studied up well on hoochie coochie
Lick lips, kitten with a whip so undress me, undress me

Hey, pretty pretty with the sweet sweet eyes
Order me up another slice of your pie

Whiplash, I never looked at you in high school
Hot child, always walk behind you for the rear view
Good god, baby, baby blow my fuse
When you walk this way
Nineteen seductive ballerina so trashy, trashy

Hey, pretty pretty with the sweet sweet eyes
Order me up another slice of your pie
(Sixx & Mars, 1989)

If the anatomical metaphor of "pie" was too subtle here, Warrant's 1989 song "Cherry Pie" spawned a video in which, in addition to shots of firehoses being sprayed and a buxom young woman in a tightly fitting waitress outfit, there is a close up shot of a piece of cherry pie falling into the lap of the aforementioned young actress (Warrant, 1989).

From Poison's first hit, "Talk Dirty to Me" from their 1986 debut *Look What the Cat Dragged In*:

> You know I never
> I never saw you look so good
> You never act the way you should, but I like it
> And I know you like it, too
> The way that I want you
> I got to have you, oh yes I do
> You know I never
> I never ever stay out late
> You know that I can hardly wait, just to see you
> And I know you cannot wait, wait to see me too
>
> Cause baby, we'll be
> At the drive-in, in the old man's Ford
> Behind the bushes till I'm screaming for more
> Down the basement, lock the cellar door
> And baby, talk dirty to me
> (Dall, et al., 1986)

Their next album, 1988's *Open Up and Say...Ahh!* featured another hit, "Nothin' But A Good Time":

> Now listen
> Not a dime I can't pay my rent
> I can barely make it through the week
> Saturday night I'd like to make my girl
> But right now I can't make it through the week
>
> I'm always working, slaving, every day
> Gotta get a break from the same old, same old
> I need a chance just to get away
> If you could hear me think this is what I'd say

Don't need nothin' but a good time
How can I resist?
Ain't lookin' for nothin' but a good time
And it don't get any better than this
(Dall, et al., 1988)

Although tamer than the Mötley Crüe and Warrant sentiments about women, there is a decidedly misogynistic and utilitarian view of both women and sex in the Poison lyrics. Poison's tours were promoted with sexual indulgence by the band as on an equal par with the music (Spheeris, 1988; Konow, 2002), perhaps compensating with misogynistic behavior where their lyrical content fell short.

Other examples of the hypermasculinity evidenced by misogynistic lyrical content may be seen in Faster Pussycat's name, and from their 1987 debut album (Faster Pussycat, 1987), their songs "Bathroom Wall" with the lyrics "I got your number off the bathroom wall" (Downe, 1987a); and "Cathouse" which speaks of visiting an establishment known as the "best Cathouse in town" (Downe, 1987b). L.A. Guns' 1988 debut (L.A. Guns, 1988) features song titles such as "Sex Action" and "Bitch is Back" (which is not a cover of the Elton John song).

Finally, Guns R Roses earned a deserved reputation for upping the ante in Metal Glam's attitude, theatrics, substance abuse, and as a target for criticism. From their 1987 debut (Guns N Roses, 1987) *Appetite for Destruction*'s "It's So Easy":

Ya get nothin' for nothin'
If that's what you do
Turn around bitch I got a use for you
Besides you ain't got nothin' better to do
And I'm bored
(Adler, et al., 1987)

Little needs to be added here.

In addition to lyrical content, there are also images from album artwork and videos. The L.A. Guns *Cocked and Loaded* (L.A. Guns, 1989 cover will be referenced here (see Appendix 2) with attention to the image of a gun as a thinly veiled phallic symbol, especially a cartoon woman is straddling the weapon. The inner fold of Guns N Roses *Appetite for*

Destruction features a Robert Williams painting of the same title (see Appendix 2), depicting the aftermath of a robotic rape scene. This was intended to be the cover of the album, although Geffen records executives thought better of it (Neely, 1992). From video sources, we have already referenced Warrant's "Cherry Pie" video, but Mötley Crüe's "Looks That Kill" video (Mötley Crüe, 1986) will be mentioned as within the narrative of the video, a group of scantily clad post-apocalyptic women are corralled by a fence as the band plays in their teased hair and make-up. Later in the video a woman warrior figure threatens to free the women and is fought by members of the band in a science-fiction/Satanic battle.

These themes of women as sexualized objects, violence against women, and women as a threat are indeed pervasive in Heavy Metal in general and Metal Glam in particular (Walser, 1993; Weinstein, 2000). This therefore leaves us with the question of what meaning we can take from a genre in which men appropriate attributes of the feminine in the service of not just masculinity, but of hypermasculinity, perhaps going as far as misogyny. How are we to understand the clash in elements represented in the icon of the Metal Glam androgyne? What sense do we make of a popular culture genre which takes the appearance of the feminine in the service of the masculine, or at least a version of the masculine?

Context: The Audience - Demographics: Age, Gender, Race, Geography

The extreme clash of elements of the masculine and feminine in Metal Glam is interesting enough. However, our problem of focus here becomes all the more interesting when it is placed into the context of the audience for Metal Glam of the 1980s, an audience that was predominantly young, male, and grappling with developmental tasks of individual as well as sexual identity development.

Authors Walser (1993) and Weinstein (2000), a musicologist and sociologist, respectively, gathered comprehensive data on the composition of Heavy Metal audiences from marketing, sales, concert attendance records, and other demographic sources. Despite slight variation in the actual figures cited by the authors, there is an agreement of an age range between 12 and 18 (with ages 11 and 31 as extreme outliers) as the predominant Heavy Metal audience (Weinstein, 2000, p. 99; Walser, 1993, pp. 16-17). This age range lowers the ceiling as the broader genre of Heavy Metal is specified into the sub-genre of Metal Glam (also referred to by the above authors as *lite metal,* or *glam metal*), the result that audiences for Metal Glam tend to be "uniformly adolescent" (Weinstein, 2000 p. 110). Based on this data, we may then consider the audience age range to be somewhere between 12 and 18. This age range was also supported by Klosterman's (2002) memoir of coming of age in the "hair band" era, as his narrative begins at roughly this age (Klosterman reports himself to be in the fifth grade when coming into possession of his older brother's copy of *Shout at the Devil*).

Both authors noted the racial and ethnic composition of Heavy Metal (and therefore Metal Glam by extension) to be predominantly white in the early 1980s and becoming progressively racially and ethnically diverse by the 1990s. This is mirrored by the racial and ethnic composition of the performers, who, until the late 1980s were almost entirely white. The authors also agree on the demographics of middle class as the predominant audience. Some movement toward upper-middle class is noted toward the late 1980s as Heavy Metal became the dominant popular music genre, yet both authors also agree on a working-class ethos embedded into the culture and forms of expression of Heavy Metal in general. Walser (1993) cites Billboard marketing surveys which note "blue-collar industrial cities of the U.S.", as well as other surveys which noted "upscale family suburbs" (Walser, 1993, pp. 16-17). Certainly by the late 1980s, the geography of Heavy Metal was diffuse and pervasive:

> By 1989, heavy metal accounted for as much as 40 per cent of all sound recordings sold in the United States, and *Rolling Stone* announced that heavy metal now constituted the mainstream of rock and roll. (Walser, 1993, p. 3).

Klosterman's (2002) memoir supports this by citing *Billboard* charts for any given week in 1987, in which "[t]here were between twenty and twenty-five metal bands on the *Billboard* Top 200 chart", and further, that "[I]n the 1980s, heavy metal *was* pop (and I say that to mean it was "*pop*ular" (Klosterman, 2002, p. 4). Further, both Walser (1993) and Weinstein (2000) note that Metal Glam was the most marketable and therefore most visible and pervasive form of Heavy Metal.

Given the popular status of heavy metal toward the end of the 1980s, it is safe to assume that most areas of the U.S. were represented.

The question of gender balance remains. Weinstein (2000) and Walser (1993) both cite a more even gender distribution toward the end of the 1980s, yet they also cite the very uneven gender balance of the early

33

1980s: "At least until the mid 1980s, heavy metal was made almost exclusively by male musicians for male fans" (Walser, 1993, p. 76). Walser continues:

> Heavy metal is, inevitably, a discourse shaped by patriarchy. Circulating in the contexts of Western capitalist and patriarchal societies, for much of its history metal has been appreciated and supported primarily by a teenage male audience (Walser, 1993, p.76).

Weinstein's (2000) research also notes Heavy Metal's predominantly male following. Weinstein frequently refers to Heavy Metal as not only masculine, but masculinist:

> Whereas other youth cultures and audiences, such as the early 1970s glam rock following that coalesced around David Bowie, and the mid-1908s pop audience for Culture Club and Michael Jackson, countenanced play with gender, heavy metal fans are deadly earnest about the value of male identity. Masculinity is understood in the metal subculture to be the binary opposite of femininity. Much like the religious fundamentalism that denounces heavy metal, the metal subculture holds that gender differences are rooted in the order of things: it is perilous even to question, let alone breach, the boundaries (Weinstein, 2000, p. 104).

Given the gender balance which is reported as predominantly male, as well as the hypermasculine lyric and image presentation cited above, one might ask how we are to make sense of the stereotypically feminine attributes of the Metal Glam androgyne. Although, the question entails more than just the clash in masculine and feminine elements played to a white, middle class, geographically pervasive audience. The youth of the audience, especially given the previous citations of early adolescence becomes an important factor in our question, and the importance lies in the developmental tasks that a male adolescent or pre-adolescent audience would necessarily be engaged in. The developmental tasks referred to here would be the tasks of peer group identity formation, individual identity formation, and sexual or gender identity formation. The developmental eras of pre-adolescence and adolescence are seen as crucial stages in these

34

areas of development (Blos, 1962, 1979; Erikson, 1963, 1964, 1968, 1979; Kohlberg, 1966, 1969, 1984; Kohlberg & Zeigler, 1967; Lasky, 1993).

The connection between the developmental tasks of pre-adolescence and adolescence and a popular medium whose identifying markers are androgyny and transgressive sexual presentation becomes more meaningful in light of the importance placed on music and peer culture.

The idea of music and popular culture having an impact on youth culture should not come as a surprise. One need not go back as far as the birth of Rock and Roll, record burnings in the South, or the FBI's close examination of the lyrics of Louie Louie in 1956 (Deane, 1995; Gaspin, et al. 2000). With some degree of regularity there are court proceedings or public outcry concerning the influence of Rock and Roll on America's youth. Tipper Gore's Parents' Music Resource Center brought such a concern to Senate hearings in the mid 1980s, charges of subliminal messages in Judas Priest and Ozzy Osbourne songs were levied in the wake of teen suicides, and within the past five years the aftermath of Columbine High School has raised concern and pointed fingers in the direction of groups Rammstein and Marilyn Manson as well as the Basketball Diaries film (Manson, 1999; Gaspin et al. 2000).

Aside from the sensationalistic headlines and extreme and tragic events referred to above, there is some merit to the idea that popular culture plays an important role in pre-adolescents and adolescents. Weinstein (2000) cited a 1984 survey which resulted in 81% of 12 to 18 year olds reporting music as an important part of their lives. Walser (1993) reflects similar statistics. Additionally, Kinney's (1999) investigation into peer subculture reviews the psychological literature from 1949 to the date of publication which underscored the importance for youth of membership in peer groups, including "deviant subcultures" (Kinney, 1999). As Kinney's research interest was adolescent Heavy Metal peer culture, his findings may be considered to be generalizable to this work. Additionally, Rosenblum (Rosenblum, et al. 1999) frames popular culture as a projection screen for adolescent tasks of development.

Aside from the importance of popular culture and the developing adolescent, we have the questions of why a highly sexually charged, potentially gender-bending, androgynous, misogynous, and oft riotous popular entertainment form plays a role in the development of a particular subset of preadolescent and adolescent males, who are largely White and largely middle-class. Questions arise as to the meaning of misogyny for this population. The possibility of "gender anxiety" comes to mind in reflection upon an art form that takes the tropes of femininity to use in the service of a rigid and "traditional" masculinity. The parallel to the Drag Queen show as interpreted by Paglia (1992) and Butler (1990) where femininity is not imitated but lampooned is called to mind. A connection between the "gender anxiety" and women threatening the social order of men and therefore masculinity, as depicted in Faludi's (1999) account of the Citadel military school, including the cadet's frequenting of Drag shows, is linked to Metal Glam's "boys only" code while makeup is being applied and heels are being strapped on. The significance of the tasks of development in preadolescence, grappling with identity and sexuality, appear to be writ large in popular culture as Metal Glam is seen as a reflection of American Culture in the 1980s grappling with social and historical changes that challenge former definitions and identities of the concept of "masculine".

In summation, we are left with the cultural and historical phenomenon of Metal Glam, which appeared in 1983 and dissipated by the 1990s, a more exacting history will follow in the next chapter. Metal Glam became a dominant force in popular music by the end of the 1980s, attracting a geographically widespread audience, although predominantly in the pre-adolescent and adolescent 11-18 age group. The fact that Metal Glam appealed to a predominantly preadolescent audience, at a stage in which individual and gender identity developmental issues are assumed to be prevalent, and given that this cultural genre traded as heavily in gender representation should have been of greater interest to psychology.

Despite an interest in gender studies beginning with Constantinople's pioneering work in sex role identification (Constantinople, 1974), a body of work encompassing androgyny and identity largely identified with the work of Sandra Bem (1974, 1981, 1984, 1987a/b; Bem, Martyna, & Wilson, 1976), the connection between Metal Glam and adolescent gender identity formation surprisingly has been left untouched by psychology. The two extant sources for exploration of Heavy Metal and issues of gender identity, Walser (1993) and Weinstein (2000) have been referred to extensively in this chapter.

Additionally, the historical and cultural aspects of 1980s Metal Glam have also been neglected. While Weinstein (2000) concerns herself with the sociological dimensions of the Heavy Metal audience, the social organization of forms, the transmitted values and transgressive politicality of Heavy Metal, and while Walser (1993) examines semiotic issues of

36

power, gender, and madness within the lyrical context as well as structurally within the music itself, there has yet to be a pulling together of the social and cultural histories which culminate in the 1980s. Essentially, it will be the work of this paper to examine the cultural construct of masculinity using Metal Glam as an historic benchmark of masculinity in transition during the 1980s. Although prior to this, we must locate Metal Glam within an historical context within the larger genres of Heavy Metal and Rock and Roll.

Chapter II: Tracing the History of Metal Glam

This chapter will define Metal Glam: what constitutes Metal Glam, and where Metal Glam is located in history. The musical genre of Metal Glam will be stringently defined as to the elements of the genre, including the semiotics of style, sound, and lyrical content. Also delineated here will be the historical era under consideration. Metal Glam will be defined as a formal style, documented by the release of albums noted as significant in the genre. In this chapter, it is be important to locate Metal Glam in history, not just in its prime, but to trace its antecendents. This will move in two converging directions.

First, the history of Heavy Metal will be traced to its formal roots in Black Sabbath and the resulting New Wave of British Heavy Metal (often cited as inspiration by Metal Glam artists). The exploration of Heavy Metal will also look at the foundations of Heavy Metal, the proto-Metal of blues inspired rock and roll, psychedelia, and biker culture, which positions Altamont as the historical turning point for Heavy Metal and its culture.

As Metal Glam is critically understood as a hybrid of Heavy Metal and British Glam, the history of British Glam will also be briefly examined, tracing these roots back to David Bowie, Marc Bolan's T-Rex, Gary Glitter, Roxy Music, and what is often referred to by critics as the "mascara revolution" of the early 1970s. This history will briefly look at the legacy of gender as transgression in the avant garde and will touch upon Surrealism, Dada, The Romantics, and other benchmarks in artistic history.

Chapter One has already introduced Metal Glam as a Heavy Metal subgenre and introduced some of the historic key works of the genre. The following will define how Metal Glam is constituted as a genre, how it is differentiated from the larger genre of Heavy Metal, and how Heavy Metal defines itself in contrast to the larger musical genre of Rock and Roll. As Metal Glam is something of a hybrid between the genres of 1970s Heavy Metal and 1970s British Glam, we will have to present Metal Glam in its historic context, as the product of these two musical cultures.

To quickly delineate the history, Heavy Metal starts with the first Black Sabbath album in 1970, becomes formalized as a musical genre by 1979 with the rise and recognition of the New Wave of British Heavy Metal, and in 1982-1983 splits into two directions: Metal Glam and Speedmetal or Thrash Metal. British Glam emerges formally in 1972, peaks artistically in 1974-1975, and then becomes mainstream throughout the later 1970s, until revived by Metal Glam in 1982-1983.

What Is This That Stands Before Me?[x] Heavy Metal History as a Social History

Before embarking on a journey of Rock and Roll's dark brother and secret sharer, Heavy Metal, it would be well to preface such an exploration with a few words about the use of a popular culture such as Rock and Roll as a social and historical text.

Rock and Roll may be more complex than meets the eye or ear. Behind the roar of the greasepaint and the smell of Teen Spirit are social, economic, political, and ideological factors. Just as the history of Science (Science with a capital "s" to indicate Science itself as a metadiscipline) is no longer conceptualized as a better idea replacing an older one found to be less good, Rock and Roll is neither conceived of as one form coming in to replace another form in a purely linear fashion. Just as the history of Science is moved, shaped, and constructed by numerous external forces, so is Rock and Roll. As an extended example, to refer to David Bowie's 1969 hit "Space Oddity" as a meaningless pop novelty song is to ignore the social climate of the Space Race of the 1960s, and concomitantly to ignore the deeper political implications of the Space Race, namely the ideological battle for World Supremacy at the end of the Cold War. Additionally, that Bowie is British finds another layer in that the question is raised as to whether the song's protagonist, Major Tom, reflects the impotence of a once great nation, no longer a World Power, now reduced to a cultural figurehead. Further, the technological implications of extraterrestrial anomie are heightened when the context of Woodstock-era folkism is brought into the frame, as this was the musical genre context of Bowie's 1969 *Space Oddity* album. Finally, an adolescent pop market audience must also be brought into this context as the song's Major Tom drifting from Ground Control may well reflect a developmental stage of subjective aimlessness, confusion, and search for grounding values and identity.

It would be premature to dismiss "Space Oddity" as a meaningless pop novelty song, as suggested above by the cultural, social, and historical richness with which it is seeped. Indeed, any pop song (or Heavy Metal song, Punk song, Glam song, or Metal Glam song for that matter) is rooted in a social and cultural history, and this is why the tracing of Metal Glam's history is necessarily difficult, dense, confusing, and convoluted, as we shall soon see. It is much like tracing the history of the Psychoanalytic

movement, where we can draw a straight line backward from Freud to Breuer, and backward again to Charcot and Janet, and backward again to Mesmer. But this leaves out Nietzsche and Dostoevski, whose phenomenological writings likely had a deep impact on the maturing Sigmund. This also leaves out hydraulic model, rooted in positivistic physical science. This also leaves out the energy system model Freud grafted onto the hydraulic model. Further, this leaves out the classicism inherent in Freud's Greek Mythological reference points, which point to a Neo-Classical Renaissance at Turn of the Century Vienna, complete with tarot cards and an Occult revival. The social (and sexual and moral) history of Vienna is left untouched by the straight lines, as are Freud's identity as a Jew is Catholic Vienna, as is Vienna's relation to the Western World.

This example of the complexity of Psychoanalytic history serves as illustration: although straight lines are tempting, there are too many pieces left out. A similar complexity in tracing the course of Metal Glam's history may also be noted. In terms of Metal Glam, it would be tempting to draw two straight lines from Mötley Crüe backwards to Black Sabbath and Marc Bolan's T.Rex. But this leaves out Judas Priest, Slade, the Sweet, the Sex Pistols, the New York Dolls, Elvis, the Beatles, Surrealism, and the Church of Satan, all of which play a part in the history of Metal Glam. Although straight lines are easily drawn, they leave out a wealth of information. It may be more accurate to draw a pentagram…

Important Musical Context

Sorcerers of Death's Construction[xi]: Black Sabbath and the First Wave of Heavy Metal

Both Walser (1993) and Weinstein (2000), in their definition of Heavy metal as a genre note that like any artistic or intellectual genre, there is never complete agreement about what it is that constitutes Heavy Metal, or perhaps more importantly, who are the members of the metal pantheon. Both writers, however, concede that there is a fair amount of agreement about who is in the pantheon and who is out. The following historical outline is based on the consensus of record labels (as culled from liner notes and genre categories cited by the labels), artists, and music critics.

Just as Psychoanalysis traces its lineage back to late 19th Century Vienna, and the meeting of Josef Breuer and Sigmund Freud, with an acknowledged pre-history of Charcot, Janet, and Mesmer, as well as a literary undercurrent of Nietzsche, Dostoyevski, and Poe; Heavy Metal

40

also identifies a lineage for itself. The genre of Heavy Metal recognizes its formal genesis at the release of Black Sabbath's 1969 self-titled debut album. Black Sabbath would become the band that all other bands that defined themselves as Heavy Metal would consistently cite for their inspiration (Black Sabbath, 1994, 2000). Black Sabbath's debut contained all the sonic and thematic characteristics of Heavy Metal: blues based, centered around the guitar riff, distorted guitars, tight precision, dark themes, and simple arrangement of drums, bass, guitar and vocals.

Essentially, Black Sabbath *is* Heavy Metal. That first album set the tone and defined the sound for all else to follow. As Bergmann (1993) notes post-Freudian extenders, modifiers, and heretics, the same will follow for post-1970s Heavy Metal bands who either stay true to the Black Sabbath sound and themes, those that expand upon the original template, and those that break away from these founding fathers of metal. The Black Sabbath sound is synonymous with Heavy Metal. It is a sound typified by distortion, heaviness, fullness, simplicity, and control that veers into chaos. The music itself is blues-based, formed around Delta blues chord progressions of I, IV, V. This is typical of most of Rock and Roll, but as the Rock and Roll of the late 1960s and early 1970s began to merge folk and jazz improvisation into Rock and Roll (most notably the work of Beatles which incorporated Bob Dylan's folk base, and the West Coast post-psychedelia such as the Animals and the Doors, who would blend free-form post-be-bop jazz stylings into blues-based rock and roll (Deane, 1995), the music that became Heavy Metal would stay closest to the Delta blues roots of artists such as Muddy Waters, Howling Wolf, Johnny Lee Hooker, and other legendary bluesmen (Walser, 1993).

Heavy Metal is traditionally organized around the guitar as a primary instrument (as opposed to Hip Hop, which would be organized around the percussive tracks or jazz or folk which are not primarily rooted around a specific instrument), which results in an emphasis placed on the virtuosity of the Heavy Metal guitarist (many of the tracks on the Black Sabbath debut album showcased Tony Iommi's guitar talents), as well as the structure of the song being organized around the structure of the guitar itself. This may be noted in the scales and runs found in the Heavy Metal of the formative 1970s, the root open E chord, and use of blues structured call-and-response riff style. The riff is prominent in Heavy Metal. Essentially a riff is a music phrase consisting of a root note and a repeated run, this is the essence of Heavy Metal, this is the hummable, the

41

Comes back to the idea that HM is a "Blues" music (see p8)

whistleable, the memorable musical phrase of the song, essentially, a Heavy Metal song is formed around the riff.

The rich influence of the blues in Black Sabbath is supported by liner notes for the first album, which note that prior to their incarnation as Black Sabbath, the foursome of Osbourne, Iommy, Butler and Ward were a blues band called Earth (Black Sabbath, 1970). Also indicative of the blues influence are the lyrical content of the occult and supernatural, which Walser (1993) traces back to Robert Johnson's epic blues tales of salvation and damnation.

The strong connection to the blues is not unique in Rock and Roll as basic Delta Blues song structures may be seen in 1950s Rock and Roll pioneers Chuck Berry, Little Richard, Bo Diddley, and Fats Domino. What happened in Heavy Metal though was that the blues backbone of Rock and Roll became heavier and deeper than the Rock and Roll of the 1950s and the 1960s.

Get Your Motor Running[xii]: Heavy Metal's Prehistory

To place this in historical and geographical context, British Rock and Roll of the 1960s was experiencing a blues revival. The R&B early works of the Beatles and the Rolling Stones which sparked the British Invasion of the Kinks, Dave Clark Five, and a host of English bands also lead to a new generation of English youth discovering the blues. Among these were Jimmy Page, Jeff Beck, and Eric Clapton. Aside from being among the most critically acclaimed musicians of their generation, Page, Beck, and Clapton each served time in the Yardbirds, a British Blues Revival band of the mid 1960s. This will be important in the history of British Glam, to be discussed later in this chapter, but also for the development of Heavy Metal, as the Yardbirds would allow for the formation of Led Zeppelin, Cream, and the Jeff Beck Group, each featuring experimental guitar pyrotechnics which would become the lifeblood of Heavy Metal.

The Delta Blues influence in the Yardbirds and post-Yardbird projects of Clapton, Beck, and Page is evident, as was the gradual thickening and "heavying" of the riffs, of the tone and texture of the music. Bands such as Led Zeppelin, Deep Purple, and Cream all grew out of the post-Yardbird British Rock of the mid-1960s. This period of Rock and Roll history is often cited and referenced by Heavy Metal musicians and performers (Konow, 2002; Walser, 1993) as an essential ingredient in the evolution of Heavy Metal.

The blues-inspired British post-Yardbird scene was directly influential on the career of Jimi Hendrix, who guitar virtuosity is frequently cited by Heavy Metal guitarists. Hendrix' brand of blues-inspired psychedelia, like the post-Yardbird projects of Beck, Clapton, and Page, also focused on the guitar, the riff, and a "heavying" and "loudening" of the music, which Walser (1993) observes was only possible with technological advances in amplification, specifically and amplification in the low end of the sonic spectrum, the bass, thereby adding the "heavy" to Metal.

Hendrix, Led Zeppelin, Deep Purple, and Steppenwolf are frequently cited by Heavy Metal musicians, fans, and critics as giving birth to Heavy Metal. And herein is the fusion of blues-based Rock and Roll with the psychedelia of the late 1960s, perhaps best exemplified by Iron Butterfly's *In-A-Gadda-Da-Vida*, a 17 minute sprawling and chaotic sonic romp which may be considered influential to Heavy Metal in the use of primary instruments (guitar, bass, and drums), the heaviness of the sonic tone, the call-and-response riff structure, as well as the extended guitar and drum solos, which would become a standard part of the Heavy Metal vocabulary.

In addition to the musical and structural antecedents of Delta Blues and British Rock of the mid 1960s, there were social and political antecedents as well. In America, the Summer of Love of the mid-1960s gave birth to the Hippies, politically and socially liberal, and bohemian and nomadic in lifestyle. The "peace and love and joy" acoustic folk music and gently crafted bittersweet vocals were not embraced by all. There was an undercurrent, a dark side to the flowers and beads of Haight-Ashbury. Politically this was seen in fringe and radical groups such as the White Panthers, the Chicago Seven, and the growing ranks of the Hells' Angels (Deane, 1995). Historically this was seen in the melee at the Rolling Stones concert at Altamont Speedway, where Biker culture formally clashed with Hippie culture resulting in death. Rolling Stone rock critic Greil Marcus cites Altamont as the official end of the Summer of Love (Deane, 1995), which opened the gates for a nativity in black: Heavy Metal.

Musically, there was also a counterculture to the Hippie Haight-Ashbury culture. Three of the most prominent of these were Iggy and the Stooges, the MC5, and the Alice Cooper Band. All three were from Michigan, and all three wove darker imagery and more nihilistic themes into their music. Where the Hippie culture preached peace, these bands

43

sang of violence. Historically, this is a turning point in that these three bands would influence important future directions in Rock and Roll. The MC5 and Iggy and the Stooges would become inspirational forces for an American Punk Rock movement in the Ramones, the Cramps, and Television, which would then infect England's Sex Pistols and the Clash. Additionally, Iggy Pop himself would directly influence 1970s British Glam movement under the wing of David Bowie. Finally, the Alice Cooper Band would coalesce under the personality of their lead singer, Vincent Furnier, who would adopt the band's name as his own and become a prominent figure in proto-Metal Glam (Konow, 2000; Weinstein, 2000; Hoskyns, 1998; Deane, 1995).

To contextualize Alice Cooper's gender-bending moniker, the reader will be reminded that popular music had been pushing the envelope of gender norms in fashion and behavior since the British Invasion in 1964. Hair was getting longer, fashions were becoming unisex, boot toes were pointier and perhaps more feminine while heels were getting higher. The sentiment that the gender of a young person was unrecognizable until closer inspection was commonplace beginning in the early sixties, and perhaps continued to the post-hippie era. Additionally, the Vietnam protest movement and the gathering calls of "Peace, Love and Understanding" and "Give Peace a Chance" may represent a shift to a more feminized organization under the Age of Aquarius. In this light, Alice Cooper becomes significant as a benchmark of shifts in gender presentations in his long hair, his unisex attire of lame, vinyl, and leather jumpsuits, platform shoes, eye makeup, and of course, his name. Alice Cooper also becomes significant historically as representing, along with Black Sabbath, the darker side of the late 1960s, the inverse of the "Summer of Love".

So there was a dark and disturbing undercurrent to the flowers, beads, and rainbows, and this undercurrent was largely industrial and urban, and these bands paved the way for a heavier and darker music brewed from a danker and more dismal version of Detroit: Birmingham, England, the birthplace of Black Sabbath, and later Judas Priest and a host of other Heavy Metal bands. Birmingham would become a Metal Bethlehem.

Seasons of Whither[xiii]: The Early Sounds of Heavy Metal

The starkness and severity of the opening chords of Black Sabbath's debut album reflected the environment of Birmingham. Osbourne, years later, would reflect on the dismal themes and occult fantasies as the product of an English industrial town, stating that their futures felt bleak to them, and this was injected into the lyrics and themes (Moll, 1999). The starkness and bleakness of Birmingham was also reflected semiotically and structurally in the minimalist arrangement of drums, bass, guitar, and vocals. The tone of the album could be described as both "dark" and "heavy", and the tempo could be described as "thick" and "plodding". All these elements conjure imagery of a post-modern industrial wasteland. The thickness and heaviness of the tempo was commented on by Boston Globe music critic Jim Sullivan, in his 1980 review of Black Sabbath's "Heaven and Hell" album when he noted that one could bang one's head in time with the bassline and sustain only minimal injury.

So in 1970 the first Black Sabbath was unleashed upon the world. The album was not expected to sell well by the executives at Warner, and it was not critically acclaimed (Black Sabbath, 1998). With little to no label support *Black Sabbath* became a highly sold record, generating a loyal fan base. This was the birth of Heavy Metal. Although, at this point, as the genre of Heavy Metal was in formation, there was no clearly defined genre. Instead, Black Sabbath was associated with bands that shared a blues-base, dark themes, and loud distorted guitars. By the mid 1970s, the term *heavy metal* began to be used as a descriptor:

> The term "heavy metal" has been applied to popular music since the late 1960s, when it began to appear in the rock press as an adjective; in the early 1970s it became a noun and thus a genre. (Walser, 1993).

Walser also notes, as he traces the history of Heavy Metal, that the genesis of the term likely derives from Steppenwolf's lyric "heavy metal thunder" in "Born to Be Wild" (often covered by Heavy Metal bands), William S. Burroughs' *The Ticket That Exploded* (Walser, 1993), connotations for chemical poisoning via *heavy metals*, as well as the phallic imagery inherent in the phrase "man of heavy metal", pertaining to guns and armory (Walser, 1993).

Although Walser cites the use of the term "heavy metal" in the early 1970s, this was too early for the designation of a genre. More typically, a band that played loudly and aggressively would be categorized as "hard rock", perhaps to differentiate the band's sound from contemporary popular music such as the Carpenters, the Mamas and the

Papas, the Association, Carole King, Joan Baez, and James Taylor, all of which were considered to be Rock and Roll. Bands such as Aerosmith, Kiss, Angel, the Blue Öyster Cult, Thin Lizzy, Deep Purple, Foghat, and Led Zeppelin had a significantly different sound, different lyrical themes, and a different fan base. The term "hard rock" set these bands apart from their abovementioned "soft rock" colleagues. Some of these bands are considered to be Heavy Metal, like Kiss, the Blue Öyster Cult, and Thin Lizzy, and certainly Kiss and the Blue Öyster Cult, as active bands in the 1980s, attempted to identify themselves in the Heavy Metal genre. Although, as mentioned above, in the early 1970s the genre of Heavy Metal was still in formation and there was little cohesion in terms of the musical style, lyrical content, thematic content, or the style of the band's image. The members of Black Sabbath note that they simply considered themselves to be a Rock and Roll band, and frequently experienced difficulty fitting in with other bands on tours and fitting into radio formats (Black Sabbath, 1998, 2002; Moll, 1999). It is also interesting that although Kiss aligned themselves with the formal genre of Heavy Metal in the mid 1980s, spokesmen Paul Stanley and Gene Simmons have always referred to themselves as a Rock and Roll band (Kitts, 1994; Lendt, 1997).

As an example of the different musical styles of the bands considered to be the "first wave" of Heavy Metal, Aerosmith's sound is reminiscent of the Rolling Stones, riff-heavy, although their beat, their central organizing rhythm borrows heavily from John Lee Hooker's blues-boogie meter. The Blue Öyster Cult, despite the liberal use of the umlaut, was more reminiscent of blues-based psychedelia, complete with harmonies and jazz inspired complex guitar runs than what today would be considered Heavy Metal. Kiss' wardrobe, presentation, fire-breathing, blood-spitting, stage sets, and pyrotechnics may have been inspiring to future Heavy Metal musicians[xiv], but their music itself (1973 to 1980 catalog) has more in common with the Beatles than with Black Sabbath: songs are roughly 3 minutes, vocal harmonies are carefully constructed, and the production is quite slick and polished (which will be necessary elements for Metal Glam, to be extolled ahead). Not only was Heavy Metal not *Heavy Metal*, but the classification "hard rock" was not uniform nor unifying. Heavy Metal did not yet have a look, a sound, a structure that would serve to identify itself with. This would change by the end of the 1970s.

Hell Bent for Leather[xv]: The Second, or New Wave of British Heavy Metal

Birmingham was once again Bethlehem. The industrial cities and towns of the English countryside[xvi] spawned Judas Priest, Iron Maiden, Mötörhead , UFO, and Diamondhead, among numerous other bands. These bands identified themselves as Heavy Metal from their outset[xvii] and their sound was more uniform than the bands lumped under the category "hard rock" in the early 1970s. This new, self-consciously styled Heavy Metal, identified as the New Wave of British Heavy Metal (or NWOBHM by the music press: Metallica, 1998; Walser, 1993; Weinstein, 2000), featured the sonic force of Black Sabbath merged with the vocal power of Led Zeppelin's Robert Plant. The NWOBHM featured dark themes, dark lyrics, lyrical content concerning violence, the occult, alienation, suffering, and crises in identity, all seeds planted by Black Sabbath. The guitar sound was a thick, bright distortion, tightly controlled and synchronized, often two lead guitars intertwining complex phrases, thunderous drums and a solid floor of bass guitar. Over this tightly controlled cacophonous din wailed the banshee-cry of the lead vocalist (hardly ever considered to be a "singer"), liberally borrowed from Led Zeppelin's Robert Plant's falsetto pitch piercing the wall of Jimmy Page's guitar.

The NWOBHM represented more of an artistic movement, a group of musicians working independently on common themes with a unifying presentation, much like the artistic movements of Surrealism or Dada. This was different from the early 1970s where the sound and lyrical themes of Black Sabbath (demonic possession and paranoia, generally speaking) were very different from the sound and lyrical themes of Kiss (sex and the healing powers of Rock and Roll, generally speaking). Under the NWOBHM, Iron's Maiden's Satanic sonnets were more consistent with Judas Priest's technological terrors, which were consistent with Mötörhead 's WWI imagery, and again consistent with Diamondhead's apocalyptic atmospheres, bringing us back to Satan. It was under the NWOBHM that imagery not specifically associated with a singular band came to represent the genre of Heavy Metal. Satanic imagery, skeletal imagery, medieval weaponry and torture implements, gothic backdrops and demonic bestiaries all came to represent the genre of Heavy Metal. It was at this point in time that a band could put a skull or occult symbol on their album cover to designate themselves as a Heavy Metal band[xviii].

Yes There Are Two Paths You Can Go Back But in the Long Run[xix]: The Split in Heavy Metal

Following the New Wave of British Heavy Metal, the "second wave" which served to organize the genre around sonic, visual, and thematic guidelines, the "third wave" of Heavy Metal was American, and largely centered in the West Coast. Musicians who comprised this "third wave" of Heavy Metal frequently refer to first and second waves as their direct inspiration, yet what is interesting about this third wave is that following the crystalization of the genre in New Wave of British Heavy Metal, the genre splits into two camps in the third wave. One camp was Metal Glam, which took the sound and the intensity of the New Wave of British Heavy Metal yet moved Heavy Metal into a more marketable, more slickly produced, more vocally polished direction. Additionally, an element of glamour was added to Heavy Metal's leather and studs "bad boy" look: performers wore make-up, clothing became visual loud and garish, and there was a feminine quality to the overall presentation. In short, Metal Glam represented a fusion of Heavy Metal and British Glam of the 1970s (to be discussed shortly). Metal Glam identified itself with Heavy Metal, although the movement was met with much derision, as may be seen in the derogatory terms such as "poodle rock", "poseur rock", or "lite metal" (Walser, 1993; Weinstein, 2000; Klosterman, 2002a).

The second camp of the Third Wave of Heavy Metal was not differentiated with a name or descriptive title in its time, although is presently referred to as Speed Metal or Thrash Metal, and was essentially the polar opposite of Metal Glam. While Metal Glam was image conscious and focussed attention on wardrobe, make-up, hair, and accessories, Speed or Thrash Metal became almost consciously style-less, and the attractiveness of the band members could actually be a liability in Speed or Thrash Metal[xx].

Oh, You Pretty Things[xxi]: 1970s British Glam

The dyed roots of 1970s British Glam are not as uniformly agreed upon as those of Heavy Metal. Some look to Elvis' mascara and gold lame suits as the first hints of Glam, others suggest the long hair of the Beatles and other British Invasion bands as the first outing of the Glitterati. Not even the denominator is universally agreed upon as Hoskyns (1998), music critic for London's *Mojo*, cites both *Glitter* and *Glam* being used synonymously to identify the form.

The term *Glitter* derives from Gary Glitter, the self-given stage name of performance artist Paul Gadd: Gary Glitter. Gary Glitter's claim to fame was the 1972 hit "Rock and Roll Part 2", a continuous guitar riff followed by a chorus of "Hey!", still played at baseball games nationwide. Gary Glitter became identified with the genre of *Glitter Rock* or *Glam,* due to his stage attire of shiny silver suits, extreme make-up and high platform heels. Many critics and historians would cite Gary Glitter as codifying and unifying Glitter Rock under one name, one riff, and one rhythm (Hoskyns, 1998).

The term *Glam,* on the other hand, refers perhaps to the earlier Glam roots of T.Rex and David Bowie, especially with an ear to the mysticism expressed in these artists. *Glam* is short for glamour, which ostensibly refers to the attire of the artists as it expresses a highly stylized presentation. In addition to referring to glamour as in fashion, it also refers to the Scottish root of *glamour*, meaning to blind or dazzle one's opponent thereby spell-binding them (Pfister & Sharg, 1997). In fact, music critics would cite that the image, dress and presentation of Glam had an equally spell-binding effect on its fans.

Glam artists of the 1970s were known for outrageousness in presentation, particularly leaning to transgression of sexual norms and mores through expressions of homosexuality or bisexuality, hypersexuality, and androgyny. This was achieved through dress: elaborate materials, shiny or glittery, very feminine for the early 1970s, perhaps growing out of a unisexual Woodstock/post-psychedelic era. Shoes were platforms, the higher the better, hair was not only long (as long hair was symbolic of the hippie revolution, a dissent from the status quo) but now styled and coifed, teased and colored, and make-up was mandatory. The presentation of the male musician in the Glam genre of Rock and Roll was androgynous, but more than simple androgyny, the presentation was that of a transgressive sexuality. It wasn't enough for the Glam genre to simply incorporate stylistic elements of the feminine in wearing long hair as the Beatles did in 1965-66; it wasn't enough to merely push the envelope in a neo-Brummel fashion as did the mods from 1966-68; and it wasn't enough to don new garb that did not have traditional gender-roles ascribed to it, like the hippies' ponchos and tie-dyed. No, for the Glam artists, the shock of their sexuality and androgyny was part and parcel of the Glam aesthetic.

For the most part, it was the *look* of a band that distinguished it as Glam. This may be tied to the expanding medium of television and print in the late 1960s and early 1970s, and also the advent of color television in

Hyperculte

the 1970s, which bore out the loud and garish colors of Glam to their fullest dayglo effect. England's television programs such as *Top of the Pops* became the showcase for new music in the early 1970s, and many British Glam artists and music critics cite appearances on *Top of the Pops* as defining moments for a band's image (Hoskyns, 1998), and the show became as important as radio was for the Beatles and the Rolling Stones in the mid 1960s. Also, this was a time when visual stylists entered the roster of the recording industry[xxii]. The result of this, as a lesson learned from Elvis and the Beatles, that the image of a band or performer was instrumental in *selling* the artist. Another lesson learned along the way, perhaps from the Rolling Stones, was that transgression could also be helpful in selling a product.

The lesson that 1970s British Glam took to the bank was that sexuality was transgressive, and that sex sells. Elvis' pelvic gyrations from the 1950s were shocking in their time, the suggestive lyrics of the Rolling Stones were also shocking in their time. By 1970, the Sexual Revolution and Women's Movement were in full swing, suggestions about sex and sexuality were not enough to be shocking anymore, now the ante had been upped and sex and sexuality needed to be transgressive to be shocking. One way this was achieved was through ambiguity, another, building off the first, was androgyny. Male performers dressing "pretty" was shocking in its sexual ambiguity as well as in the ambiguity of sexuality. The wearing of make-up, earrings, tight pants, glittery, shiny garb, sequins and scarves, high heels and platform boots, these were all shocking in their ambiguity of sexuality. More than just the wardrobe, though, was the performance: Glam musicians began to preen and prance, stage behavior became sultry, seductive, slinky, and oft salacious.

The use of sex, sexuality, and sensation around sex and sexuality to be transgressive and therefore part of the "shock" element of art was not invented by British Glam, or even the Rolling Stones or Elvis. No, there is a long history of the use of sex and sexuality either consciously as a shock tactic by 20th and pre-20th Century artists. Deeply embedded in the tradition of the avant-garde is the tradition of moving counter to the collective norm for a variety of functions. Most introductory Art History classes make note of Manet's *Olympia*, Dada and Surrealism's use of sexually suggestive referents, and onward to the debate over Mapplethorpe's photography to point to the use of sex and sexuality (and ambiguous sexuality) as shocking within the context of its time, serving a particular function for the art in question. Beyond the visual and plastic

50

arts, Joyce's sexual puns, D.H. Lawrence's wrestling scenes, Miller's *Tropic of Cancer*, and the banned works of Beats Burroughs and Ginsberg are surveyed in most modern literature courses to raise the issue of the function of sex and sexuality as shocking, again within the context of its time, and again serving a particular function. Finally, a brief review of television and the cinematic arts, from the twin beds of Dick Van Dyke and Mary Tyler Moore, to the "one foot on the floor" rule of Hollywood, through Bertolucci's *Last Tango In Paris* up to current debates on the V Chip and Blockbuster sanitization of cinema, will also point to the use of sex and sexuality as shocking within the context of its time, and again serving a particular function. Whether the function of depicting, referring to, or suggesting sex and sexuality is to explore sex and sexuality as aspects of the human condition or simply as shocking in its "forbidden fruit" capacity, there is a long history of sex and sexuality as transgressive with the arts, and perhaps more so in the avant-garde tradition, which typically is further on the edge of culture, on the edge of acceptability. We will see more as we work our way through the brief history of 1970s British Glam.

Before There Was Rock You Only Had God[xxiii]: David Bowie and Marc Bolan, the Romulus and Remus of British Glam

The initial point of entry for British Glam is widely considered to be the 1970 T.Rex single "Ride a White Swan". Rock critic Hoskyns (1998) claims that this single was chronologically the first to capture the Glam aesthetic. The movement of Glam, however, as documented by the Glam singles[xxiv] really starts in 1972. In fact, following T.Rex' 1970 "Ride a White Swan", there seems to be a void until 1972 when a veritable Glam explosion ushers forth hits from Slade, the Sweet, David Bowie, Lou Reed, BeBop DeLuxe, Gary Glitter, and Mott the Hoople. Glam would then run until roughly 1975-76 when British Punk came in as an antithesis to British Glam.

The roots of Glam seem to go back to David Bowie and Marc Bolan's T.Rex (Hoskyns, 1998). As a Delta Blues influence was a common theme to the First Wave of Heavy Metal bands, it would seem that a folk influence is the common strand between Bowie and Bolan.

Bolan's pre-Glam incarnation carried the moniker Tyrannosaurus Rex, and the group was essentially a duet: Marc Bolan and Steve Peregrine Took. Took's role was equivalent to that of Art Garfunkle's, as percussive sidekick, playing tambourine or bongoes as Bolan strummed an acoustic guitar and sang Tolkein-inspired ballads[xxv]. These albums had the influence of Bob Dylan and Donovan, merging folk sounds and song structures with psychedelic references. By 1970's *Beard of Stars* LP, however, Took was replaced by Mickey Finn, and the new duo shortened their name to T.Rex and crafted the hit "Ride a White Swan" and changed their format to electric (as cited in liner notes to T.Rex, 1971). The following year, T.Rex rode the success of their white swan on *Top of the Pops* and other showcases as the song was a hit in both England and America.

It was with the *Electric Warrior* album that T.Rex defined their new sound. Hoskyns (1998) frames Glam as being simultaneously retro and futurist, and this description works quite well for T.Rex. Here we have a musical form that is based on the blues, and therefore referential to the past, which is reinforced by Bolan's medieval mysticism in songs like "Mambo Sun", "Cosmic Dancer", and "Planet Queen", yet a decidedly futurist spin is found in Bolan's Glam attire as well as various modernist themes such as Jaguar and Cadillac cars, velvet hat fashion statements, ray guns, and flying saucers.

The sounds and visions of T.Rex would also be set forth from the *Electric Warrior* era. After 1970's "Ride a White Swan", the T.Rex attire became more glittery and more extravagant. Hoskyn's cites as a defining moment in Glam history Bolan's wearing make-up on *Top of the Pops* (Hoskyns, 1998) and frames this as an event which caused a Glam revolution, setting Bowie's Ziggy Stardust in motion along with Slade, the Sweet, and a host of other Glam bandwagonners. Bolan's garb transformed from hippie-era faded denim to gold and silver suits, sequins and sparkles. Also, his performance became more sexually seductive, and this became a hallmark of the Glam sound. Bolan's voice was sultry and seductive; he would modulate his tone from a quiet controlled come-hither beckoning whisper and build to raspy vocal ejaculations, hoots, and howls. This vocal style would also be heard in David Bowie's Glam era, as well as The Sweet, Slade, and BeBop DeLuxe. Essentially, the vocal style set forth in *Electric Warrior* would become a vocal signifier of Glam.

Other sonic signifiers of Glam that would have their precedent set in the *Electric Warrior* album were the drum and guitar sounds. Hoskyns (1998) identifies the drum sound as "compressed" and "mechanical" sounding (Hoskyns, 1998, p. xii). The drum sound to *Electric Warrior* and the 1972 follow-up *The Slider* does have a compressed sound, slightly muted and taking a secondary background position to the guitars and vocals, which formed the foreground. Drums, bass, and rhythm guitar all formed a tightly knit unit in Glam, much more cohesive than the traditional Rock and Roll of its time where a looser connection in the rhythm section may be noted. This tightness and cohesion in the rhythm section, beyond Hoskyns' simply noted drum sound, became another signifier of 1970s British Glam.

The guitar sound, again, having been set as precedent in *Electric Warrior* is distinctive and a signature Glam sound. The guitar sound is characterized as "fat", "heavy", and "thick" (Hoskyns, 1998). Note that these adjectives were also used to describe the sound of Heavy Metal. The distinguishing characteristic of the Glam sound, though, was a "sweetness" or "slickness" of the guitar. The riffs tended to be light, airy, and boppy as opposed to Heavy Metal's dark, dense, and dangerous sound. Whereas Heavy Metal used distortion sonically to represent power through overdrive (Walser, 1993), Glam used light distortion and reverb through tube amps to give the riffs a slightly wet quality. These musical signifiers helped suggest seductive sexuality as opposed to the primitive power evoked by the power chords of Heavy Metal. Also, as noted in Bolan's vocal style of modulating from control to chaos as a musical metaphor for sexual abandon, the guitar sound also captured a sensation of control in the tight riffs that would veer out of libidinous control. This was often the function of the guitar solo, as an ejaculatory expansion of the main theme or phrase of the riff. Compared to Heavy Metal, where the guitar solo serves as a virtuoso showcase, as an expression of mastery and declaration of dominance (as suggested by Walser, 1993; and Weinstein, 2000), the guitar solo in Glam was more embedded into the main riff and had more of an ornamental role.

Finally, the last signature sound of the Glam genre was the simple sing-along chorus. For example, the chorus to the biggest hit from *Electric Warrior*, "Get It On (Bang a Gong)" (Bolan, 1971) was represented in the title of the song in its entirety. Other choruses in the album were equally simple: "Jeepster"'s chorus was "Girl I'm just a jeepster for your love" (Bolan, 1971). Later T.Rex songs would follow this formula of a single phrase repeated as the whole of the chorus. As Glam would evolve over the next four to five years, the simple sing-along chorus would become a staple, as would be later seen in The Sweet and Slade's infectious and superficial catchphrases.

As mentioned above, the twin sources of Glam were Bolan's T.Rex and David Bowie's reinvention of himself as Glam icon Ziggy

Stardust. Although Bowie's pre-rock career was informed by theatre and show tunes, both of which were incorporated into the Glam aesthetic. Bowie's pre-Glam incarnation was identified with a Woodstock era folk ethos.

By the late 1960s the style that had been settled on was Dylan-inspired folkster. Bowie's hair was long and unruly, he played acoustic guitar and sang of wild-eyed boys from "Freecloud", extraterrestrial visitation during a free festival, and other themes that bordered on the mystical, much like his contemporary Marc Bolan.

The mix of retro and futurist that Hoskyns cites as fundamental to Glam (Hoskyns, 1998) was more evident in Bowie's musical style than his lyrical content as was the case with Bolan. Bolan's retro elements, aside from his mysticism-inspired lyrics, were essentially his blues-based riffs and stripped down format of guitar, bass, drums, and vocals, the raw essence of rock and roll itself, referring back musically to Chuck Berry, Elvis, and the early Rockabilly and Blues roots of Rock and Roll. Bowie was a more complex artist than Bolan and was able to experiment more both musically and lyrically, therefore, Bowie was able to go beyond Rockabilly retro referents and incorporate classical, jazz, and Music Hall elements while simultaneously pushing the envelope in more experimental compositions. The *Aladin Sane* and *Pin Ups* albums capture Bowie's retrofuturism in original compositions such as "Drive In Saturday" or "The Prettiest Star" which are essentially doo-wop structured ditties packaged in modernist arrangements that communicate a plastic prefab quality. Also from these two albums are Bowie's covers of Rock and Roll standards, such as the Rolling Stones' "Let's Spend the Night Together" and The Who's "Can't Explain". These songs, which by the 1973 recording date, were already embedded into popular consciousness, akin to duChamp's "readymades", were given a postmodern Glam treatment by Bowie in updating these traditional pieces to the new slick, sweet, and seductive sound of Glam.

The album that ushered Bowie into Glamdom, though was 1972's *The Rise and Fall of Ziggy Stardust and the Spiders From Mars*. The 30th Anniversary Edition compact disc booklet documents Bowie's reinvention of himself from denim post-Woodstock folkie to space-age flamboyant androgyne. With the *Ziggy Stardust* album Bowie's musical style changed with the introduction of The Spiders From Mars, as guitarist Mick Ronson, bassist Trevor Bolder and drummer Mick Woodmansey, and their sound, like Bolan's, moved from acoustic strummings to standard Rock and Roll arrangements with the Glam signature drum, guitar, and rhythm section sound, as illustrated in the T.Rex section above. Another element to drastically change was Bowie's look, which, like Bolan's transformation, was more flamboyant, more outrageous, and more theatrical than previously. While Bolan would be satisfied with eye make-up and glittery attire for stage appearances, Bowie completely transformed his image (see Appendix 2): his long hair was cut, shaped, and sculpted into a futuristic design: Rock historians would credit Bowie with the inspiration for the Punk aesthetic). Bowie's make-up moved beyond highlighting his natural features to expressionistic design[xxvi], and his attire was not traditional clothing that had been accented with flamboyant flourishes, but was essentially costuming reminiscent of Picasso's Perrot era, a Nijinski production, or science fiction comic books.

Onstage Bowie behaved in a sexually seductive as well as sexually ambiguous manner (Pennebaker, 1984; Deane, 1995). Part of the live act to gain notoriety was when Bowie appeared to be performing fellatio on guitarist Mick Ronson during a solo[xxvii]. Bowie's appearance was not simply androgynous, it was so hypersexual and so sexually ambiguous as to be regarded as alien[xxviii] (Bowie, 2002; Hoskyns 1998).

Lady Stardust Sang a Song of Darkness and Dismay[xxix]: Lou Reed's post-Velvet Glam Flirtations

Lou Reed is something of an instrumental figure in 1970s British Glam while at the same time being something of a peripheral figure to the movement. Reed's band from 1966 through 1969 was the Velvet Underground, a band that merged styles of jazz, blues, folk, and psychedelia into its own New York West Village hybrid. Reed has reluctantly acknowledged some of the credit for the Velvet Underground to Andy Warhol, who sponsored and featured the band as a regular fixture in his Factory, his Exploding Plastic Inevitable Pop Art installations and other assorted "happenings" in the latter half of the 1960s New York art scene (Marcus, 1989).

After Reed left the Velvet Underground in 1969, he was courted by David Bowie and supported by his record company (RCA, Bowie's label) while living in London to record his first solo album (Hoskyns, 1998; Bowie, 2000, McNeil & McCain, 1997; Reed, 1972). Bowie's interest in Reed had to do with his strategies for reinvention as an alien Glam androgyne as Bowie saw in both Reed and Iggy Pop (also sent to London at this period to write material for Stooges records) something very American that Bowie sought to tap into for his own benefit in the overseas markets (McNeil & McCain, 1997). Reed, for his part, had appeared to embrace some of the look and the sound of the emerging Glam aesthetic.

Reed released two Glam-oriented albums in 1972. The first, self-titled, was essentially a collection of leftover Velvets material with a few new songs. The arrangements, however, were more lush than the minimalist Velvets, and the inclusion of R&B/Soul back-up singers gave the album a retro feel that fit in with the emerging Glam aesthetic. Reed's second album of 1972, *Transformer*, however, bore the official stamp of Glam not only in its title being highly suggestive of transgressive sexuality, but also in production credits: David Bowie was listed as the producer. *Transformer* also became a seminal Glam album in its content, much of it driven by Warhol-related material which had become a point of fascination to the growing Glam culture. Also in this album was Reed's only Number One hit "Walk On The Wild Side", which recounts a narrative of cross-country elective gender reassignment, as well as photos of Reed in drag on the back cover. The sexual ambiguity helped cement *Transformer* into the Glam canon.

The Ballroom Blitz[xxx]: The Sweet, Slade, Mott The Hoople, and BeBop DeLuxe

As in any movement there are primary shaping figures and there are peripheral figures. In Rock and Roll there tend to be innovators who begin movements or styles, and others who take that style as a vehicle. In the case of 1970s British Glam, the innovators were Bowie and Bolan, with Lou Reed as an inspirational figure for Bowie. The "extenders", to use Bergamnn's (1993) notion of post-Freudian thought, of Glam were bands like The Sweet, Slade, Mott the Hoople, and BeBop DeLuxe, bands that bandwagonned onto Glam and attained pop notoriety. Generally, bands of this nature do nothing more for the genre than flesh out the pre-existing themes and styles, they add little innovation and do little to bring the genre forward.

The Sweet was essentially a British pop band of the early 1970s. They were fortunate to have professional songwriters Nicky Chinn and Mike Chapman working for them. After Bolan's and Bowie's Glam annunciations, The Sweet were photogenic enough to refine their image in high Glam style complete with silver and gold lame suits, high platforms and silk scarves. The Sweet's sound fit well with the Glam aesthetic, the guitars were well controlled giving way to momentary spurts of constrained chaos, and their vocalist's style of seductive and sultry crooning could quickly modulate to unbridled utterances of rapture, moving several octaves to suggest sexual ambiguity. The pop sensibilities of Chinn and Chapman may have helped push Glam into popular culture as The Sweet's material was as infectious and catchy as a commercial jingle, which is essentially the goal of the pop song. Their hits "Ballroom Blitz" and "Fox On The Run" made the Glam movement more visible.

Slade was another British band of the early 1970s that had only achieved vague acknowledgement until changing from skinhead style to Glam. Slade's version of Glam was less sexually ambiguous and more fashion-oriented toward stylistic outrageousness. Slade's platforms were tall, their suits shiny, and their plaids and stripes loud. Slade was essentially a flash-in-the-pan pop sensation that penned memorable songs such as "Gudbye to Jane" which would later be covered by Britny Fox, and "Cum On Feel The Noize" which would be covered by Quiet Riot, ushering Heavy Metal into the mainstream at the outset of the 1980s.

Mott The Hoople, in contrast to Slade, had more musical promise and more musical diversity. Mott The Hoople began as a straightforward Rock and Roll band, mixing Dylan's folk stylings with the grind and drive of the Rolling Stones. Legend has it that the band was about to hang up their guitars when David Bowie offered them his freshly-written opus "All The Young Dudes", which quickly became a Number One hit for Mott The Hoople (Hoskyns, 1998). Mott The Hoople's members would wear make-up, and their fashion sense bordered on Glam, including platforms, sequins, and scarves, although by the mid-1970s this was standard Rock and Roll attire.

Perhaps the band that did the most to push Glam into its next phase was Bill Nelson's BeBop DeLuxe. Formed in 1972, the band did not release its first album until 1974. That album, *Axe Victim* has been critically acclaimed as exemplifying the high point of Glam, as well as representing a high-water mark for Rock and Roll itself. The combination of lush production, thematic content, musical virtuosity, and picturesque album art marked the beginning of a new era in Glam, one to be dominated by Brian Eno's early albums, Roxy Music, and Queen. These bands, along with BeBop DeLuxe, represented something of a baroque period in Glam, where the composition became more sophisticated (a case in point being Queen's chamber music arrangements, and in particular "Bohemian Rhapsody"), the imagery more romantic, and the references more literate.

57

similar style of crossing to Glam metal

Glam metal meted away from this.

Glam was moving away from the pop stylings of The Sweet and Slade, and had moved away from the edgy sexuality of Bowie's Ziggy Stardust, and even further away from Bolan's visceral virtuosity and retrofuturism. Glam would become High Art in popular culture, the stage productions would become more lavish, the recording procedures more perfectionist, the wardrobes more lavish and less garish, and the egos of the performers more bloated. This evolution in Glam gave the brewing Punk movement plenty to react and revolt against. *Core*

Shock Me[xxxi]: The New York Dolls, Alice Cooper, and Kiss

The history of Rock and Roll is replete with movements and trends communicating back and forth across the Atlantic: Elvis inspires the Beatles and Rolling Stones who in turn inspire American Pop and Bubblegum, which in turn inspired British Glam (Deane, 1995). The back and forth of expressive and receptive is not necessarily a one to one correspondence but perhaps one of mutual evolution: Glam in American looked, sounded, and connoted differently from its British counterpart. Glam was also not as widespread or as cohesive in America. For instance, Alice Cooper has been considered to be lumped into the Glam category, although his music bore none of the Glam signature sounds. Alice Cooper's music had more in common with American Hard Rock or First Wave Heavy Metal. The guitar riffs were prominent, there was a blues base, and the lyrical content had to do with adolescent angst and alienation. Alice Cooper's name was sexually ambiguous, and the fashion style of the band incorporated platforms, scarves, and other outrageous accoutrements, and there was a sense of the theatric in the performances. However, there was more of a shock element to Alice Cooper, and the stage show themes were horror-themed, as his lyrics took a bent toward the macabre. There was very little retrofuturism in Alice Cooper and the increasingly macho posturing of the band left very little to connect with the British Glam scene. Alice Cooper was, however, emerging at exactly the same time as British Glam, his band was formed in the late 1960s, and they experimented with sounds and styles before hitting upon their shock-rock style. It is interesting to note however, that Alice Cooper is considered to be among the canon of early Heavy Metal (Weinstein 2000), and was considered to be associated with Glam at the time (Hoskyns, 1998), this would stand Alice to be among the progenitors of Metal Glam. His name rarely comes up in these circumstances, though. For instance, when Mötley Crüe founder, Nikki Sixx, cites his influences, Alice is

58

revered, although left out of the equation that went into the formation of Mötley Crüe (Strauss, 2002).

Also developing along the lines of Alice Cooper in the mid-1970s was Kiss. Kiss' use of theatrics, costuming, stylized appearance and painted faces conceptually aligns them with British Glam, however, as in the case with Alice Cooper, the macho posturings of the band were not consistent with British Glam sexually ambiguous presentation, with the exception of lead singer Paul Stanley. Stanley's stage presence, lipstick, and sexualized stage movements are generally overshadowed by the other band members whose posture is flagrantly heterosexual. In addition, most of Kiss' song catalog is conceptually based around the male sexual conquest, and much of the lyrics misogynist. This was not consistent with the British Glam aesthetic of sexually ambiguous, seductive, and sexualized presentation, although these will be important elements to keep in mind as Metal Glam proper evolves.

The New York Dolls were really the only American band to transplant the British Glam aesthetic onto American soil. In their career only two albums were formally released. The first album, released in 1974, depicts the band in drag (see Appendix 2), full make-up, and many members in high heels. This was the first taste of American home-grown Glam. The New York Dolls met several of the criteria for British Glam: their sound was blues-based, stripped down retro three chord numbers, occasional doo-wop references were noted, their look was androgynous on album covers and in concert, their lead singer, David Johanson, modeled himself after Mick Jagger and would behave in a seductive, salacious, sexually ambiguous manner. The music, however, although being retro, was too sloppy and spontaneous to *feel* as though it were categorically related to bands like T.Rex, The Sweet, and Slade. They were closer to Mott The Hoople, who were on the fringes of Glam anyway.

Like the Velvet Underground, the New York Dolls are frequently cited as influential to a number of bands, yet in their time they did not achieve widespread popularity. Glam did not take off in America as it did in England. The various reasons and meaning behind this cannot be dealt with at present[xxxii]. Additionally, Glam in America was translated as horror-shock (Hoskyns, 1998) or as the lead-in to Punk (McNeil & McCain, 1997). Glam would have to wait roughly ten years and be fused with the masculinist ethos of Heavy Metal in order to be revived.

God Bless the Children of the Beast[xxxiii]: Van Halen, Quiet Riot, Twisted Sister and Mötley Crüe

With the end of the New York Dolls and the advent of Punk in the late 1970s we end the history of 1970s British Glam. This history now collides with the history of Heavy Metal that we left off at the end of the New Wave of British Heavy Metal, also at the end of the 1970s. So it would appear that two forces were brewing in Britain: one of Glam and one of Heavy Metal. In America Glam had given way to Punk. In addition to the rise of Punk in America in the late 1970s, the New Wave of British Heavy Metal had reached the shores of America along with Heavy Metal from other countries, such as Australia's AC/DC and Germany's The Scorpions and Accept. This in turn inspired American Heavy Metal in the form of bands like Van Halen, Quiet Riot, and Twisted Sister.

While Van Halen achieved almost instantaneous success thanks to critical acclaim for guitar virtuoso Eddie Van Halen, marketing, and their ability to fuse pop sensibilities with Heavy Metal stylings. Van Halen's cover of Kinks' classic "You Really Got Me" was the hook for the album. This new rendition of a time-honored Rock and Roll staple was in the same strategic vein as Bowie's Glam covers of traditional standards and allowed Van Halen to appropriate the already existing popularity of the song, thereby achieving their own popularity. It helped that Van Halen's original material and individual musicianship could match the success of that first single.

A similar career trajectory is noted in Quiet Riot, whose first hit single was a cover of Slade's "Cum On Feel The Noize". Quiet Riot, unlike Van Halen, were not able to live up to their earlier success. What they did achieve, along with Van Halen, though was bringing Heavy Metal into the mainstream Top 40 radio.

The Heavy Metal sound was becoming the cultural currency of the early 1980s. Other developments included Ozzy Osbourne leaving Black Sabbath and achieving success (as well as radio airplay) as a solo artist, increased popularity for New Wave of British Heavy Metal bands like Judas Priest and Iron Maiden, as well as increased popularity for other imported Metal such as AC/DC and the Scorpions.

Kiss had also finally attained recognition in 1978 and were able to carry this with them into the very start of the next decade, and Alice Cooper had also made a name for himself. But these performers, who would have been thought to have been the first wave of Metal Glam did not have as much influence in the new genre as Twisted Sister.

60

Twisted Sister followed the typical Rock and Roll success story: they slogged it out in bars and clubs while experimenting with their format until hitting upon a formula that took them to fame. For Twisted Sister, the formula was Glam. Essentially, they were a Hard Rock band looking to provide more of a "draw" to their live shows. Their tactic took Alice Cooper and Kiss one step further, or rather one step backward, into Glam style (see Appendix 2). Lead singer Dee Snider and the band would wear full make-up and a more aggressive footballesque version of Bowie's alien androgyne garb. Rather than the "prettiness" that is associated with Metal Glam of the mid-1980s, Twisted Sister presented as garish, cartoonish, and menacing in their interpretation of Glam. Their transgressive look was consistent with their anti-authority lyrical rhetoric, and at the very turn of the decade in 1980, Twisted Sister found themselves at the top of the charts.

Prior to 1983, the elements of Metal Glam had been put in place. In addition to Twisted Sister's costumed theatrics and make-up, Van Halen's David Lee Roth presented as seductive, sultry and sexualized, the back cover to the first album suggests lipstick and eyeshadow dripping from his sweaty face. Quiet Riot, although not known for wearing make-up, were among the first Heavy Metal bands to wear spandex and sport stylized guitars painted with broad stripes or concentric circles (see Appendix 2). These were all Glam-like and paved the way for bands like Mötley Crüe and Poison who were self-consciously Glam.

1983 marks the release of Mötley Crüe's second album, *Shout At the Devil*, and with this record, both the sound and look of the band, Metal Glam formally enters Rock and Roll history. Although the first album had a very British Glam sound to it, suggested by tight rhythm sections, simple sing-along choruses, compressed drum sounds, T.Rexesque guitar riffs, and song arrangements reminiscent of Mott The Hoople (particularly "Public Enemy Number One" and "On With The Show"), the black and white photography of the cover did not capture Mötley Crüe 's early Glam leanings (see Appendix 2). Further, the front cover focus on Vince Neil's crotch too closely recalled the Rolling Stones's *Sticky Fingers* cover (see Appendix 2) to be associated with British Glam (Klosterman, 2002a), and the inner photo of the group posed underneath an inverted pentagram banner heightened the references to Black Sabbath's Satanism while the lack of color downplayed their make-up. Essentially, Motely Crue were a Glam band playing to a Metal audience, although the Glam nuances of their presentation and the polishing on their music did not come to be

61

recognized until the second album in 1983. It could also be speculated that without the precedent of Quiet Riot's spandex and striped outfits, without Van Halen's sexualized frontman, and without Twisted Sister's alien androgyny, audiences would not be ready for Mötley Crüe until 1983.

If we are to claim that the release of *Shout At The Devil* constitutes a new genre in Rock and Roll, the genre of Metal Glam, we need to define this genre in its looks, sounds, and themes, as we defined the genres of Heavy Metal and British Glam.

So, what is it about the 1983 recording *Shout At The Devil* that identifies it as the entry point of Metal Glam? We have already identified Mötley Crüe's first album *Too Fast For Love* (Mötley Crüe, 1981) as being musically referential to British Glam in certain elements. The drum sound and guitar sound have been noted, but also is Vince Neil's voice, a high pitched falsetto, which is not immediately identified as masculine and therefore sexually ambiguous, meeting some of British Glam's criteria. Another element of this first album are the names of the performers, the adopted stage names. While stage names were not exclusive to British Glam (case in point Richard Starkey renaming himself Ringo Starr), the Dickensian stage name emerged with British Glam. Names such as Ziggy Stardust, Aladin Sane, Gary Glitter, and Freddie Mercury (nee Farrakh Bulsara) all have celestial or glamorous connotations[xxxiv]. Stage names for Mötley Crüe members Nikki Sixx and Mick Mars appear to be a hybrid of Glam and Punk sensibilities as guitarist Mick Mars' has celestial connotations while Nikki Sixx is both sexually ambiguous and refers to Satanism's Number of the Beast 666. Later Metal Glam monikers would be either sexually ambiguous or refer to an element of danger as a signifier of Heavy Metal as in the example of L.A. Guns guitarist Tracii Guns. These stage names are not unlike the use of the stage name in the Drag Queen circuit.

Aside from the above Glam referents, in the first album we have referents to Heavy Metal in the garb of the band. This includes leather pants (precedent being set by New Wave of British Heavy Metal band Judas Priest, see Appendix 2), the guitars held by band members (Weinstein, 2000 cites appearance of guitars as signifying of Heavy Metal), particularly the BC Rich Warlock on the ground and the Explorer model held by Nikki Sixx, adorned with concentric circles (see Appendix 2). Additionally, while the drum and guitar sounds referred to the sound of British Glam, and although several arrangements were reminiscent of Mott The Hoople and T.Rex, there were also significant Heavy Metal musical signifiers, such as quickly played scales and runs (Walser, 1993; Weinstein 2000) and aggressive tempos on "Live Wire", "Piece Of Your Action", and "Too Fast For Love". Additionally, the umlauts in the band's name make references to both Mötörhead and the Blue Öyster Cult. Also, Dökken and Krökus, Heavy Metal bands briefly preceding Mötley Crüe, had used the umlaut, therefore making the umlaut itself a signifier of Heavy Metal. And as mentioned above, the inverted pentagram, along with the Gothic props of skulls on spikes and burning candles, referred to the Occult themes in Heavy Metal.

Essentially, the net result of *Too Fast For Love* is that it identified Mötley Crüe as a Heavy Metal band with Glam referents being more subtle. The 1983 release of *Shout At The Devil* would put any subtlety Mötley Crüe had to rest.

Looks That Kill[xxxv]: *Shout At The Devil* Marks the Introduction to Metal Glam

Shout At The Devil contained more overt visual as well as musical Glam referents. First, as mentioned before, the color photography on the *Shout At The Devil* cover made the band's make-up more immediately apparent. On The *Shout At The Devil* cover, lipstick, rouge, mascara, and eyeshadow are all discernable, and the sexual ambiguity affected by the make-up refers directly to 1970s British Glam. Additionally, the futuristic warrior garb worn by the band, in combination with the make-up, could place the band on the cover of a 1972-1974 era David Bowie record. This link to British Glam is also heightened by the slickness in production and sweetness of lead guitar sound: though distorted in Heavy Metal overdrive, Mick Mars' guitar sound in tone and timbre is close to that of Mick Ronson (Bowie's guitarist, also note the first name similarity) or Marc Bolan. Also closer to Glam than Metal is an overall polished sound of the instrumental tracks. The jagged, rough sounds of the *Too Fast For Love* tracks have a glossier and smoother overall sound. The choruses on *Shout At The Devil* also are reminiscent of British Glam in the simple catchphrase sing-along quality, and in fact, most of the song titles follow Bolan's title of being the entirety of the chorus (e.g., "Shout At The Devil"'s chorus is: "Shout, shout, shout at the Devil" (Sixx, 1982); the chorus to "Looks That Kill": "She's got the looks that kill, she's got the looks that kill" (Sixx, 1982); the chorus to "Too Young To Fall In Love":

Too young to fall in love

Too young to fall in love
Too young to fall in love
Too young...to fall...in love (Sixx, 1982)

And finally the chorus to "Knock 'Em Dead, Kid":

Knock 'em dead kid
Knock 'em dead
Knock 'em dead kid
Knock 'em dead
The blade is red kid
Knock 'em dead
Knock 'em dead kid
Knock 'em dead" (Sixx & Neil, 1982).

The elaborate photo spread in the album was also more referential to Glam than to Metal, as few Heavy Metal bands had as much focus on image prior to *Shout At The Devil*, but the most Glam-referential element to *Shout At The Devil* were the brief narrative tracks that opened and closed the first side of the album.

The album's opening track, "In The Beginning" recounts a futuristic tale with a post-apocalyptic backdrop spoken over an experimental soundtrack while the narrator's voice has been modulated by special effects:

In the beginning Good always overpowered the evil of all man's sins...
But in time the nations grew weak and our cities fell to slums while evil stood strong...
In the dusts of hell lurked the blackest of hates For he whom they feared awaited them...
Now many many lifetimes later lay destroyed, beaten, beaten down. Only the corpses of rebels, ashes of dreams, and bloodstained streets...
It has been written "Those who have the youth have the future".
So come now, children of the beast, be strong
And Shout at the Devil (Sixx, 1982).

64

This leads into the opening guitar chords of "Shout At The Devil", which are Metal in structure: slow, rhythmic, and held long while distortion builds, musically and structurally similar to "Smoke On The Water" or "Black Sabbath", as well as tonally similar to those songs in the overdriven guitar distortion that is held, signifying both power and tension, key semiotic elements in Heavy Metal, according to Walser (1993).

The narrative element of "In The Beginning" however also ties *Shout At The Devil* to British Glam as it recalls David Bowie's "Future Legend" introductory narrative to "Diamond Dogs":

> And in the death
> As the last few corpses lay rotting on the slimy thoroughfare
> The shutters lifted in inches in Temperance Building
> High on Poacher's Hill
> And red mutant eyes gaze down on Hunger City
> No more big wheels
> Fleas the size of rats sucked on rats the size of cats
> And ten thousand peoploids split into small tribes
> Coveting the highest of the sterile skyscrapers
> Like packs of dogs assaulting the glass fronts of Love-Me
> Avenue
> Ripping and rewrapping mink and shiny silver fox, now
> legwarmers
> Family badge of sapphire and cracked emerald
> Any day now
> The Year of the Diamond Dogs
> This ain't Rock and Roll,
> This is genocide
> (Bowie, 1974)

This then becomes the lead-in for the title track on the album, "Diamond Dogs", and the similarities are too much to consider the Mötley Crüe "In The Beginning" to be uninfluenced by Bowie's "Future Legend". Both songs introduce the "concept" of the album[xxxvi], both are post-apocalyptic in content, Bowie's most likely derived from William S. Burroughs while Mötley Crüe's more likely derived from the Mel Gibson "Mad Max" films of the early 1980s. Both are a little over a minute (Bowie's 1:05, Mötley Crüe's 1:13[xxxvii]), and both set the stage for a dark and dangerous album content. While Bowie's lyrical content is organized around an Orwellian theme of conformity, alienation, and violence and deceit wrapped in sexually ambiguous guise, Mötley Crüe's lyrical content organizes itself around Satanism, sex, violence, and themes of street life. Bowie is considered Glam due to the era of his recording, sound, and sexually ambiguous visual trappings. Mötley Crüe, with very similar album content, is linked more with Heavy Metal due to overt themes of Satanism and power, the calling cards of Heavy Metal (Weinstein, 2000; Walser, 1993). Also, *Shout At The Devil* helped Mötley Crüe establish themselves are musically more in the genre of Heavy Metal in their guitar sounds, and song structure, however, the make-up and visual trappings of the band, in addition to the musical and thematic referents to British Glam, forged a link with 1970s British Glam as noted extensively above, thereby creating a new genre of Heavy Metal as the visual references to British Glam were not acceptable to Heavy Metal's heterosexist ethos (see Walser, 1993; Weinstein, 2000).

Smokin' In The Boys' Room[xxxviii]: Heavy Metal's Heterosexist Culture
    This last point is important in considering Metal Glam as a new genre within Heavy Metal. Prior to 1983, Heavy Metal had begun to become more exclusively male, masculinist, and heterosexist (Weinstein, 2000; Walser, 1993). While early Heavy Metal, such as Black Sabbath, Blue Öyster Cult and Alice Cooper was not overtly masculinist in lyrical content or imagery, the genre evolved into more masculine oriented fantasy themes such as depictions of violence, horror referents, war themes, and depictions and characterizations of women that were then and now challenged as sexist. In the New Wave of British Heavy Metal in the late 1970s and early 1980s, these themes were expanded upon and Heavy Metal became not only more masculine, masculinist, and sexist, but also became exscripting of women, as noted by Walser (1993). By the mid 1980s the themes of Heavy Metal had become so clearly codified around sex and violence (also alienation and outlaw status, but these were not singular to Heavy Metal) that Tipper Gore's Parents Music Resource Center arose to meet what they saw as a challenge to the Youth of America.
    What is pertinent to the theme of this study is the fact that the presentation of sexual ambiguity that Metal Glam appropriates from British Glam sets Metal Glam at odds with the larger culture of Heavy Metal. The very look and appearance of the Metal Glam performers was met with resistance by the larger Heavy Metal "community" (Strauss,

2002; Spheeris, 1988; Moll, 1999; Gaspin et al. 2000). However, as the Metal Glam look and sound evolved from Van Halen, Quiet Riot, and Twisted Sister, who were by and large accepted as Heavy Metal bands, by the time Metal Glam had been codified (circa 1983-84, as noted by the release of *Shout At The Devil*), the precedent had been set and Metal Glam bands like Mötley Crüe, Ratt, and L.A. Guns could not be outright rejected by the Heavy Metal community, they were however, differentiated as another form within the larger genre of Heavy Metal. Had the musical referents in Metal Glam been striking different from Heavy Metal, Metal Glam would never have been conceptually grouped under the larger genre of Heavy Metal, but would instead have become its own musical genre. As will be pointed out in a later chapter, however, the fact that Metal Glam evolves from the masculinist and heterosexist genre of Heavy Metal is significant, especially within the historical context of the 1980s.

A further exploration of the gender differentiation in Heavy Metal and particularly within Metal Glam will be dealt with in the next chapter. At present, we must continue with the history in order to later understand gender differentiation within the historical context of the genre.

On With The Show[xxxix]: Metal Glam Catches On

As Klosterman notes in his memoir *Fargo Rock City* (Klosterman, 2002a), in the 1980s, Heavy Metal, and particularly Metal Glam, *was* popular music. Although this should not suggest that the release of *Shout At The Devil* automatically made Mötley Crüe a household name. Heavy Metal had crept into Top 40 radio starting with Van Halen's 1978 self-titled debut album on the strength of their Kinks cover "You Really Got Me". Quiet Riot also launched into Top 40 radio with their Slade cover, and AC/DC, after years of relative obscurity, were suddenly thrust onto major radio formats with the release of their 1980 *Back In Black* album. These Metal bands attaining popular status was not accident, but instead what critics refer to as the "crossover" effect. The crossover is when a genred musical form is able to literally cross over their genre into either another genre or appeal to a wider audience. Van Halen, Quiet Riot, and AC/DC were able to "cross over" from Heavy Metal onto popular radio. The songs that became hits had a certain amount of polish to them, were toned-down from the excesses of traditional Heavy Metal, and were essentially well-crafted pop songs with contagious, catchy sing-along choruses and melodies. Additionally, the songs by the three-abovementioned bands had antiauthority attitudes to them that "felt" genuine, as well as a certain "outlaw" or outsider status that proved to be a selling point to adolescent audiences. Essentially, this was the hybridization of Heavy Metal and British Glam: the pop hooks of Bowie, Bolan, The Sweet's Chinn/Chapmann and Slade's power-pop combined with Heavy Metal's spirit of rebellion and adolescent alienated angst. Metal Glam was a formula for popular success. — *Walzer*

Metal Glam would be more than hairspray and make-up generously applied, though. The pop song-writing hooks needed to be there too. This ensured the success of Ratt, who were not only "pretty" and fit some of the aesthetic of Metal Glam (see Appendix 2), but who also wrote catchy songs with a Heavy Metal sound and feel to them. Rat's debut in 1984 with *Out of the Cellar* followed closely on the cloven heels of Mötley Crüe. Just as Mötley Crüe had as many Metal as Glam referents, Ratt also presented as even-handed in their stylization of Heavy Metal with Glam packaging.

Also in the 1983-84 period, Kiss' Gothic-Shock appeared to be played out after a brief burst of success from 1977 through 1980, which included top 40 radioplay, sold out arenas and widespread marketing of merchandise in national markets. In 1983, after a series of personnel changes, Kiss took off their trademark stage make-up and reformed themselves in tight jeans, bandanas and a touch of mascara around singer Paul Stanley's eyes. By 1985 Kiss had gone Glam: the band was wearing visually loud and colorful clothing, album covers became more fashion-stylized, and their appearance was more in step with Mötley Crüe's 1985 fashion make-over (see Appendix 2). By 1987, even Gene Simmons, the group's most heterosexist and homophobic member was wearing mascara on and off-stage.

Look What The Cat Dragged In[xl]: The Uber-Glam of Poison

Poison won the distinction of "Glammiest of the Glammy" (Klosterman, 2002a) with their 1986 debut album *Look What the Cat Dragged In*. In Chapter One it was noted that the cover of Poison's debut album featured little to differentiate it from a cosmetics advertisement (see Appendix 2). On both the front and back covers, Poison identified themselves as Metal Glam with the appearance of the band. The music itself had few overt referents to the Heavy Metal genre, and while one could hear overtones of Judas Priest in Ratt, or overtones of Black Sabbath in Mötley Crüe, there was little to directly connect Poison to Heavy Metal. Perhaps the only signifiers to the larger genre were the rhythm of the guitar riffs: the fast attack and staccato pace, flourished with a flash of scale run ending in a feedback squeak, which had become a signifier of Heavy Metal established by Van Halen.

Poison had more to do with Glam than with Metal Glam. Both Walser (1993) and Klosterman (2002a) note that Poison was more pop than Metal, yet Poison became one of the largest sellers and most popular of the Metal Glam bands of the 1980s. Poison would take the Mötley Crüe/British Glam referents and expand them into full-fledged Glam. The make-up was more overt, the hair more styled, the fashions more contrived and conspicuous. As Mötley Crüe would codify Metal Glam, forging the hybrid between British Glam and Heavy Metal, Poison would push the Glam aspect of Metal Glam. After Posion's 1986 debut, the bands got prettier, the hair higher, while the music softer and more polished.

With Heavy Metal's heterosexist culture and lingering traces of homophobia, the gender transgression of Mötley Crüe was tolerable because they at first introduced that look along with Road Warrioresque garb and musical and lyrical allegiance to the themes and format of Heavy Metal in *Shout At The Devil*. A band as sexually ambiguous as Poison, whose music was more pop than Metal would never have been accepted into the genre without overt masculinity. What Poison was able to accomplish, though, was a "bad boy" image illustrated in songs such as "Look What the Cat Dragged In", "Blame It On You", and "#1 Bad Boy". This assertion of "traditional" masculinity allowed Poison to be successful as a Metal Glam band that didn't sound much like Heavy Metal: the lyrical themes and referents were enough to categorize them as Metal[xli].

Perhaps the most identifiable contribution Poison made to the genre of Metal Glam is that of the Power Ballad. The Power Ballad is essentially a ballad, a slow tempo song that focuses around a theme of an undying love or soulful pain, yet with overtones of Heavy Metal behind it. Led Zeppelin's "Stairway to Heaven" is often cited as an early Power Ballad as its classical beginning eventually yields to a rollicking chaotic Rock and Roll climax. Another example of an early Power Ballad is Kiss' first radio hit "Beth", which has the romantic and sensitive elements of the Power Ballad, yet none of the power of distorted guitars behind it. Perhaps the key element to the Power Ballad is the slow yet powerful chords that swell up during the chorus and especially in the final verses of the song. *Shout At The Devil* does not contain a Power Ballad, which heightens the album's association with Heavy Metal proper, as the Power Ballad is the staple of the Metal Glam band, not the Heavy Metal band. Strictly Heavy

why limit "metallic" then? Neo and "Pro-

Metal bands such as AC/DC or Iron Maiden have no slow-tempo songs, and even when a song is slowed down, the pace is menacing and plodding as opposed to the folky romantic feel of the Power Ballad. Bands other than Metal Glam have used the Power Ballad, such as Bon Jovi or Def Leppard, yet it is in the very nature of the Power Ballad's union of romantic imagery and Heavy Metal signatures that makes the Power Ballad emblematic of Metal Glam.

The Power Ballad began to appear in 1985 on Mötley Crüe's *Theatre of Pain* album with "Home Sweet Home" and hit a high point in 1988 with Poison's "Every Rose Has Its Thorn". Soon the Power Ballad became the staple radio hit for the Metal Glam band: Cinderella's big hit being "Don't Know What You Got (Till It's Gone)", Britny Fox's being "Don't Hide", Warrant's being "Heaven", and Guns N Roses cashing in on the Power Ballad formula with "Paradise City", "Sweet Child o' Mine", "Don't Cry", and "November Rain". The point being made here is that Poison was able to push the genre of Metal Glam into the truly popular domain by acting as a "crossover" band in their image[xlii], as well by their use of the Power Ballad.

By the late 1980s, with few exceptions, it was the Power Ballad that was the staple of Top 40 Radio, and this was the beginning of the death knell for Metal Glam: as the music came more into the domain of Popular Music, Metal Glam lost its association to Heavy Metal. Bands like Cinderella, Britny Fox, Extreme, and Whitesnake were known primarily for their ballads and not for the Metal elements of their sound. The look of Metal Glam had moved from the transgressive British Glam referents of Mötley Crüe's *Shout At The Devil* album to a Metal version of London's Mod/Brummel period as may be seen in bands such as Britny Fox and Cinderella (see Appendix 2).

Within the Heavy Metal community there began to be reactions to Metal Glam in the late 1980s. The reader will be reminded of the early post New Wave of British Heavy Metal split that differentiated Metal Glam from Speed or Thrash Metal. Speed or Thrash Metal began to rise in popularity in the late 1980s. Metallica's *...And Justice For All* album was beginning to outsell Top 40 bands (Walser, 1993; Konow, 2002), and bands that were entering the public eye, such as Guns N Roses, Skid Row, and L.A. Guns were moving away from their initial Glam presentation to a grimier, dirtier, and grungier look.

By way of illustration, Guns N Roses' singer Axl Rose is photographed in a collage wearing eye-make-up and sporting teased hair (see Appendix 2), yet the back cover album photo depicts a less stylized band photo. Also, the first two L.A. Guns albums depict band members wearing make-up and styled hair, yet by the band's 1991 *Hollywood Vampires* album, the focus on image is toned down, and band members are photographed in half-shadow in black and white (see Appendix 2). Finally, Faster Pussycat's 1987 debut depicts the band on front and back covers are pouting, polished, and posed, and by 1992's *Whipped!*, like the case of L.A. Guns, the bands members are not photographed in cheesecake poses.

This transformation from glamour to grungier can also be seen in our prototypic Metal Glam bands, Mötley Crüe and Posion. Mötley Crüe's glamour period becomes official with 1983's *Shout At The Devil* and runs through 1985's *Theatre of Pain*. By 1987's *Girls, Girls, Girls*, although Nikki Sixx cites a formal eschewing of his previous Glam ways (Motley Crue, 1986; Strauss, 2002; Mötley Crüe, 1986; Gaspin, et al. 2000), traces of make-up may be discerned on singer Vince Neil on the inner photo (see Appendix 2). Despite this minor detail, the look of *Girls, Girls, Girls* is less glamorous and more self-consciously hypermasculine. Decreased attention to Glam would be noted on 1989's *Dr. Feelgood* album. By 1991's retrospective *Decade of Decadence*, new videos for the band looked more in keeping with the then-cultural zeitgeist of Grunge than their early Metal or Glam roots.

Poison also toned down their Glam image from the debut album. As noted in Chapter One, Poison's first album was the more self-consciously Glam. The second album continued some Glam imagery while also depicting the band in situations and poses that were more hypermasculine (such as in front of motorcycles or sports cars, or photographed between the legs of bikini-clad women, as may be observed in the inside photo spread of the band). By 1990's *Flesh and Blood* the mascara was lost in a haze of graffiti and ripped denim, and the black and white photography on 1993's *Native Tongue* album may have been intentional to tone down Poison's past as colorful and Glam-oriented. Additionally, these inner photos depict the band members in chiaroscuro lighting and in hypermasculine poses.

Come As You Are[xliii]: The Seattle Sound of Grunge Becomes Metal Glam's Funeral Dirge

So as the 1980s end, so does Metal Glam. Klosterman (2002), in the introduction to *Fargo Rock City*, stated that Metal Glam died when Kurt Cobain appeared on MTV's Heavy Metal video program

71

Headbanger's Ball wearing a dress. This is a most astute observation for a number of reasons.

   At first, it would appear as though Cobain's presence alone were enough to throw the last handful of earth onto Metal Glam's coffin. Cobain, as lead singer and principle songwriter of the immensely popular Nirvana represents the Grunge movement itself. Nirvana was the most successful band identified with Grunge. Other popular grunge bands being Pearl Jam, Soundgarden, and Alice In Chains (who, incidentally began as a Metal Glam band yet quickly changed their sound and appearance as the tides were turning). Grunge stylistically was essentially the anti-Glam as its fashion aesthetic was flannels, tattered jeans, and blue-collar work clothes. Cleanliness and coifed hair were not among the Grunge agenda, as the name implies. The sound of Grunge also followed its visual aesthetic. It was a quilt-work of Punk, Heavy Metal, and Blues-inspired pop. The sound of Grunge was loud and un-schooled, there were no flashy guitar licks, no shiny bright colored guitars, and beard stubble replaced make-up.

   This has been noted in the shift in the appearance of Poison and Mötley Crüe from the mid-1980s through the late 1980s. Also noted were latecomers L.A. Guns, Guns N Roses, and Faster Pussycat. These bands entered Metal Glamdom just as the tides were turning from mascara to flannel. The Guns N Roses font and back album cover is very telling. The date of the album is 1987, and the tension between Metal Glam and Grunge may be noted in the above mentioned photos of Axl in make-up and teased hair juxtaposed to the back cover photo of a grimier band.

   Just a Punk Rock represented a reaction to the overly slick and bloated sound of the mid-1970s British Glam of Queen, Roxy Music and David Bowie's later incarnations, as well as the ego-heavy, studio-polished arena sound of latter-day Led Zeppelin, Foghat, Foreigner, Styx and Journey, so was Grunge a reaction to Metal Glam in all its slickness and finery. Grunge owes a musical debt to Heavy Metal in the sonic signifiers of the power chord (the principle element of the Heavy Metal craft), and the thickness and density of the riff. Grunge may be seen to have been the offspring of Heavy Metal, yet Grunge Oedipally challenged its Metal Glam patriarch in an anti-Glam sound, anti-Glam aesthetic, and anti-Glam stance on sexism.

   Prior to the release of Nirvana's 1991 *Nevermind* debut, Metal Glam bands had become Glammier, more stylized, sleeker, more made-up, and the hair was getting bigger and more teased. Also, Power Ballads were more numerous, and perhaps to balance out the sensitivity in the Power

Ballads, the lyrical content of the faster songs was becoming more raunchy. By 1989, the sexual and sexist content of the songs and videos had increased. This was the time of Warrant's "Cherry pie" song and video, which left little to the imagination. Mötley Crüe, not to be outdone in the area of gratuitous sex, released all on one album: "Slice Of Your Pie", "Rattlesnake Shake", and should there be any doubt as to the intentions of the self-proclaimed "Bad Boys of Rock and Roll", "She Goes Down" (*Dr. Feelgood,* Mötley Crüe, 1989). In writing about this period, Klosterman (2002) notes a Whitesnake video of which the song was not remembered but the gyrations of a scantily clad woman atop a car hood was.

When Grunge entered the popular culture, all of a sudden, these images of sex and sexism were no longer in vogue. This was symbolically announced Cobain's wearing a dress on Headbanger's Ball, the significance of which will be explored in full in the next chapter. What will be important to remember is that it was not the styles alone that changed, but that the styles and content of the music reflected changes in American Culture. Popular Culture reflected the changes in the larger culture, especially with regard to gender identification and gender role.

Chapter III: The Cultural Context of Masculinity

So Far, So Good, So What[xliv]: Recap and Introduction

At this point, the central problem of this project has been laid out for the reader. That question concerns the clash of signifiers that are emblematic in Metal Glam: the visual presentation of elements of the feminine juxtaposed to a hypermasculine ethos, and what possible sense one can make of this. Embedded in the larger historical context of Rock and Roll, we have seen the histories of Heavy Metal and British Glam growing from separate traditions, yet fusing in Metal Glam in the 1980s. The rise and fall of the Metal Glam empire was touched upon in Chapter Two, although the significance of the ebbing away of Metal Glam, like so much day-old mascara or flaked-away hairspray, will be shown to be informative of masculinity as a cultural construct in transition. Klosterman's (2002a) observation that Metal Glam died when Nirvana's Kurt Cobain wore a dress on MTV's Headbanger's Ball will serve as a central event of semiotic significance at the culmination of this work as gender theory and semiotics are introduced.

In this chapter, masculinity will be located as a social construct in the 1980s. This is an era in which cultural critics, historians, social scientists, and gender theorists suggest a "crisis in masculinity". In order to describe and discuss what constitutes this "crisis", the social construction of masculinity must be examined. The work of cultural historians Michael Kimmel, Anthony Rotundo, and David Savran, among others, help to illustrate the social and cultural history of masculinity and manhood in American civilization, as well as its transitions following economic, cultural, and industrial transformations which undergird the social construction of masculinity itself, according to these authors. In this chapter, I will trace the historic construction of masculinity in American culture to bring the reader through the 1980s, where the work of Susan Faludi, David Blankenhorn, and Robert Griswold, among other cultural critics, will be referred to in order to highlight and illustrate the crisis in masculinity. Essentially, the crisis in masculinity is a crisis in identity, as the song remains the same: what does it mean to be a man? As the historical context of the construction of masculinity is laid out from the 18th Century through the end of the 20th Century, what it means to be a man changes. We will see these changes as rooted in the structure of the home, the structure of the workplace, and the structure of the individual's relation to the means of production. Essentially, men move from home-centered heads of household to work-centered remote heads of household, and the status of head of household diminishes progressively with increased time and distance of the workplace demands. As workplace and domestic structures change, the demands placed on men to assimilate present as crises in masculinity. Essentially, there is a social pull for men to change along with changes in social and economic conditions, and in this transitionary period is the vacuum between what men have been taught to be, what they are, and what they are now expected to be. This vacuum is essentially the crisis in masculinity which presents itself at every cultural and historic turning point in American social and cultural history.

We could locate the first such crisis in masculinity then at the historic point of the transition from home-based guild/artisan/agrarian mode of production to industrial/factory/salesroom mode of production, locating this crisis in the mid 1800s. As urbanization and industry grow along with an urban-based population in the late 19th/early 20th Century, men are again challenged as labor removes men further from their homes and families. Additional challenges in the early 20th Century such as immigration threatened the solidarity of the White Male labor force, and as labor itself was threatened, so was masculinity. This was another crisis in masculinity, where *manhood* had to define itself in contrast to another. The call of men to arms for World Wars I and II presented another challenge to masculinity in that boys were now fatherless and overexposure to the maternal influence threatened the future of manhood in America. The repercussions of post-War America also presented men with a crisis in identity as a shift to the suburbs in the 1950s and 1960s, along with a shift in labor to from manual to managerial threatened the previously held identity of man as maker and doer. Finally, our modern era of the 1970s Women's Movement put men's roles into question, along with the Sexual Revolution, followed by economic recession, joblessness, and another wave of absent fathers and aimless youth growing up wild and uncivilized without guidance.

The crisis in masculinity shifts with each successive generation. Masculinity itself will be unpacked and presented as a fluid construct that may be seen to be tied to the relation to economy, technology, the workplace, and the structure of the family, all of which become interdigitated and embedded in gender roles and gender differentiation in juxtaposition to an other. In plain English: men were once the moral and generative head and heart of the family, shifts in the workforce shifted men out of the house more and more, wars came and went, women replaced men's functions at home and on the job, and men were left wondering how they define themselves and what does masculinity mean. This is the Crisis in Masculinity.

Also in this chapter the broader backdrop of popular culture in the 1980s will be presented as a backdrop, including Ronald Reagan's presentation of self-as-cowboy, Sam Malone's aging lothario character on the long-running sitcom Cheers, Stallone's Rambo, demographic statistics of the American family (highlighting an increasing absence in the role of the father in the home), as well as examples from children's television, such as the cartoon He-Man, Master of the Universe, not to mention the rise in Professional Wrestling.

One Of The Boys[xlv]: The Cultural History of Masculinity

The idea that masculinity is a social concept rather than an empirical entity is not unique to this work. Since roughly the 1970s, following postmodern gender theory thought, writers such as Farganis (1986), Katz (1995), Frankenberg (1993), Butler (1990), as well as the writers to be presented below, posit that gender and gender role are more functions of the social and the historical than they are functions of anatomy. The sources of this line of thought are rooted in the French intellectualism of Derrida (1991), Foucault (1973, 1980), and Lacan (1982), as well as in the American empirical psychology research of Constantinople (1974), and Bem (1974, 1981, 1984, 1987a/b; Bem, Martyna & Wilson, 1976). The psychological underpinnings of the social construction of masculinity will be further explored in the Chapter Four. For the purposes of the present chapter, we will examine the social and historical context, the determinants of the social construction of masculinity.

Running throughout the works of the authors cited below is a central theme, that historical shifts in the mode of production, technology, and the individual's relation to the economy appear correlated with shifts in the structure of the family and the home, along with shifts in gender definition and differentiation. It may be premature and not in keeping with a scientific psychology to claim that changes in the realms of technology and economy *cause* changes in family structure and gender identity, yet the correlation between changes in an economic and technological realm and changes in the descriptions and differentiation in gender roles appears to be in high agreement among the authors cited below.

Among the changes in the structure of the family is that of the father as "breadwinner" and economic head of household, shifting his role from emotional, moral, and social center (Griswold, 1993; Rotundo, 1993; Kimmel, 1996; Mintz, 1998). With each preceding shift in technology (such as the rise of the urban center of business away from the home, and the progressive shifts in automation which make forms of labor obsolete) or shifts in the economy (such as the Great Depression of the 1930s or the failure of Reaganomics in the 1980s), forces of history (such as World Wars I, II, or Viet Nam which removed men from families some temporarily, some permanently), not only did the individual's relation to the economy (literally, the person's *place* in the world), but these shifts affected changes in family structure which affected changes in gender identity and relation of one gender to another, as well as changes in the way in which the genders defined one against, or juxtaposed to another. We will see, in the pages to come, the changes in men's role in the economy and family (Mintz, 1998; Griswold, 1993), the changes in historic and social factors that serve to forge gender identification (Rotundo, 1993; Kimmel, 1996; Savran, 1998), as well as the fallout, the victims of changes (Pollack, 1998; Faludi, 1999).

And the Cradle Will Rock[xlvi]: Kimmel's Manhood In America

Michael Kimmel's 1996 opus, *Manhood in America: A Cultural History* traces the construction of masculinity through the history of technological and economic shifts. From the Genteel Patriarch landowning figure of America's pre-history, through the independent artisan, shopkeeper or farmer of America's early years, through the Self-Made Man at the Industrial Revolution, to pre- and post-War urban and suburban workers, laborers, and managers, Kimmel roots masculinity as a self-defined construct in the workforce and in Man's relation to the economy (as echoed by Mintz, 1998). Kimmel points to the 19th century, to the coining of the term "breadwinner" (Kimmel, 1996, p. 20) as the forging of the ideal of masculinity as the responsible father figure who is to provide through labor. At the heart of the masculine identity of the worker is man as useful and productive. Faludi (1999) alludes to the identity of men as workers as an identity in jeopardy, which will be discussed more thoroughly ahead.

Throughout Kimmel's research runs the thread of masculinity being threatened as breadwinning is threatened. Kimmel notes the efforts of men to forge unions, either trade unions or social unions that serve to provide solidarity and support to men, and in so doing, differentiate one group from another. The rise of the Ku Klux Klan is framed as such a men's group that sought to solidify its membership against those who were different (Kimmel, 1996). Kimmel posits that the rise in fraternal organizations, including labor unions and lodges centered around labor and the protection of the group's workers (Kimmel, 1996). Essentially, the American male worker was a White male worker, and as waves of immigration and emancipation threatened the solidarity of White male labor, the response was to band together as a united and identified whole, thereby excluding those who were different.

As history unfolds, we may witness various permutations of the theme of solidarity and exclusion, which serves to identify one group in contrast against another. Kimmel, referring to the early-to-mid 20th Century, notes that on one level, this occurs on a meta-level with the groups of work and family, that as the workplace becomes *masculinized* as men are increasingly drawn from the homes to work longer hours in factories and in urban centers (as the home-workplace is de-centered), the home becomes *feminized* (Kimmel, 1996). As the male identity moves to that of breadwinning and providing by labor outside of the home, the tasks of the inside of the home are shifted to women (Kimmel, 1996). Kimmel notes that this brings with it a "crisis" in that men are no longer socializing their children directly, they have lost central influence as emotional and moral centers of the family, and young boys are at risk for *sisification*. We can see this cultural anxiety in the 1970s and 1980s extending to the work of Robert Bly (1990) and William Pollack (1998). Kimmel suggests that this "crisis" fostered a "boy culture" as seen in the rise of the Boy Scouts and the Young Christian Men's Association in the 1920s and 1930s (Kimmel, 1996).

Throughout Kimmel's research runs the thread of masculinity rising as a conscious contrast to femininity. Masculinity differentiates itself and works against the *other*. In some cases, this *other* are competing labor pools that threaten the American Working Man, in other cases the other becomes women. We see in Kimmel (1996) the notion that boy culture is at risk for succumbing to the feminization of the home, and must be protected. In the early 20th Century, masculinity becomes placed in jeopardy and can be redeemed through the very qualities that identify boy culture, such as toughness, rough-and-tumble play, stoicism, and exclusion of women. Some of this exclusion of women also serves as solidarity in that Kimmel notes that the women's movement threatened men's jobs from the 1800s to the present (Kimmel, 1996), which further heightens the anxiety of women as a threat to masculinity.

From Kimmel's (1996) noted connection between masculinity, the workforce and the need to protect that workforce, we see the forging of masculinity in unions, lodges, and fraternal orders of the early 20th Century. Further, in Kimmel (1996) we also see a "need" to protect masculinity in its boyhood, and we see the forging of masculinity in the boy culture. It will be reminded that we are tracing the social history of masculinity in American culture, and Kimmel (1996) frames the crises in masculinity as crises in labor, the American Working Man's relation to the economy, and crises in the labor of the future, for if boys are overly feminized, they can no longer be workers as the workplace becomes identified with masculinity. These crises occur at various points through history, co-occurring with shifts in the economy, technology, demographic shifts in labor, and the changing ethnic and racial constitution of urban and suburban centers.

Boyz II Men[xlvii]: Anthony Rotundo and the Socialization of Young Men

The work of Anthony Rotundo (1993) also highlights the construction of social concepts of masculinity hinging on the relation to the economy, boy culture, and exclusionary practices to codify and define masculinity. Rotundo also underscores the notion that Kimmel (1996) alludes to, that manhood, in its historic construction, often becomes defined by a man's usefulness and his ability to produce. Rotundo also notes that the shaping of masculinity as an economic force was also fostered and forged by the socialization of boys into men.

Rotundo (1993) illustrates several transformations from the 19th to 20th Centuries. He traces a differentiation in gender marking the Victorian (late 19th/early 20th Century) era as a watermark in the codification of masculinity and femininity. Prior to the late 19th Century, Rotundo notes, aspects of the social presentation of gender, such as display of emotion, were not as sharply delineated. Rotundo notes that sculpting of attitudes toward sex, sexuality, behavior, and the home that begin to be differentiated as gender differences during the Victorian era (Rotundo, 1993). From these developments the cultural products become the social construction of masculinity as stoic, concerned with control of the passions and emotion. One may argue, although Rotundo does not implicitly, that the demands of the workplace were such that stoicism and control of the passions were of value, particularly as these qualities are thought of as the "stiff upper lip" character of Protestantism, which links Max Weber's notion of the Protestant ethic to the spirit of Capitalism (Weber, 2002). And it will also be noted that the specific responses to the specific demands of the workplace are particular to American culture, as rooted in the behavioral norms and values placed on emotion and emotional expression as part and parcel of the European heritage and emulation of gentrified classes in the newly emerging merchant class of America (Kasson, 1990).

In the new world of men being removed from the homes to the factories or salesroom floors in urban centers rather than the home, where men are no longer the emotional head of household but instead absent figureheads of economic control, childhood, boyhood, becomes sentimentalized and valued. Both Kimmel (1996) and Rotundo (1993) note the boy culture that blossoms in the 19th Century, Mark Twain is frequently cited as the hallmark of the nostalgia for lost youth, lost freedom, a wistful look back on past recklessness and rebellion (Lowry, 1997).

Rotundo (1993) notes that as important as boy culture was, as important as it was to embrace the boy as a wild uncivilized and unshod hellion, it was equally important to socialize that boy into manhood. Rotundo (1993) cites the number of boy clubs and movements that sprang up between the late 19th Century and early 20th Century to address the socialization of boys into men. Tied into this was both the notion of masculinity as "useful" and "productive", which is linked to the notion of men defining themselves as "breadwinners", but this is also coupled with the fear of a feminized youth as men were spending more and more time away from the home, as noted also in Kimmel (1996).

As in Kimmel (1996) we note the change in the relation to the mode of production, labor moves from home-based artisan, guild or agrarian to urban-based decentralized factory, salesroom or office-based profession, and men shift the role of emotional, moral, and nurturant head of household to women. Industry and urbanity figure prominently here. Rotundo (1993) notes that with this shift in the 19th Century came a certain cultural anxiety and obsession about gender. He gives as examples of this obsession and anxiety the lawyers' circuits, in which bawdy behavior was encouraged as a manner in which men could differentiate themselves from women, as a way of excluding women, thereby tightening bonds of male cohesion. Rotundo (1993) as well as Kimmel (1996) cite a number of examples of men conforming to a hypermasculine presentation of self that would include such things as avoiding ruffled cuffs and collars, the wearing of coonskin caps, the participation in frequent fistfights, boxing and other athletic activity. These activities were designated as "men only" and helped to differentiate masculine from feminine, and, Rotundo (1993) notes were helpful in socializing boys into men by teaching control of the passions, mastery over emotion.

From both Kimmel (1996) and Rotundo (1993) we see a late 19th Century/early 20th Century construction of boy culture and the cultivation of boyishness as rough and tumble, stoic, bonded, excluding of women, and socialized to be useful and purposive: "breadwinners". Certainly one may hypothesize that in the 1980s, with the confluence of elements such as the downturn in Reaganomics, downsizing and rightsizing, shifting technology, obsolete labor, and union turf wars, that a larger crisis in economy functions to uproot a sense of the masculine as the maker, the producer, the breadwinner. If masculinity is constructed to regard itself as useful and purposive, when conditions no longer allow for men to be useful the result is akin to Durkheim's normless anomie (Durkheim, 1951), where the societal guidelines that action and attitudes that previously instructed no longer apply, and the individual's meaning, behavior, and future are all cast in doubt and questioned. Essentially, men may ask "if we're not workers, then what are we?" The cultural construction of boy culture and organizations, formal and informal, intended to socialize boys to be men, has meaning in a world where the function of such goals may be fulfilled. We will see in Faludi (1999) that such boy culture and socialization of boys into men seems to fall apart in the 1980s.

Before moving ahead to the 1980s, though, Rotundo makes two observations relevant to the work here. The first is that of the differentiation between the masculine and the feminine in the late 19th Century in the area of marriage, where there is real differentiation between the roles, attitudes, and behavior of male and female in relation to one another, which begin to delineate masculine and feminine. Here we see the rise of the cultural construction of the delicacy of women and their need to be protected and sheltered, as well as their tendency to histrionics and hysterics, juxtaposed to the stoic and emotionally controlled nature of the masculine (the product of sports, Boy Scouts, and other civic activities aimed at taming the "rough-and-tumble" nature of the boy), not to mention the extension of the above to the attitudes and actions around sex and sexuality. Just as we see the socially fostered differentiation between the genders in the Victorian era, we will also see these differences or dichotomies fuse or at least move closer together by the 1970s and 1980s. This differentiation between the masculine and the feminine, however, is important to keep in mind, especially in the context of Heavy Metal's hypermasculinist nature and its exclusion of women except as temptress or castrator.

The second important point, and perhaps related, is rise of the drag show around the Victorian era. Rotundo frames this as part of the late 19th Century "obsession and anxiety about gender" (Rotundo, 1993, p. 277) and cites examples of male lampooning of femininity, or at least the outward stereotyped aspects of the feminine by all-male societies, like the Hasty Pudding Society of Harvard University. Rotundo's body of research links together the exscription of women, the exclusion of the feminine increasingly as men are progressively bounded together in the workplace. He cites the lawyers' circuits and other enclaves of men-only socialization for the workers and leaders of the future. The drag show element of the men-only enclave is framed by Rotundo as part of the anxiety about gender, and we may also read it as part of the forging of masculinity to be able to parody and lampoon the feminine in order to differentiate from it. One could make the same functional interpretation of the Minstrel Show as a manner of forging Whiteness by parodying and lampooning Blackness, by ascribing an other as different and describing that other and thereby differentiating from that other.

We do not have to venture far to Metal Glam, to point out that in the almost exclusively male and certainly masculinist culture of Heavy Metal that Metal Glam may function in a way similar to that of the drag show as Rotundo (1993) notes: as a way to further forge and unify masculinity by defining the feminine as outside, as something that is not "us". In this light, Metal Glam is not really that different from the athletic clubs, from the boys clubs, from the dirty jokes of the lawyers circuits that Rotundo (1993) delineates, or the Hasty Pudding Society as described by Rotundo (1993, despite the difference in general intellect between Harvard and the Sunset Strip). As the men-only clubs and associations of the 18th and 19th Centuries may have been ways for men and boys to work through their anxieties and concerns about gender role and masculinity and all that it entails and means, Metal Glam may also be seen as a men-only club that struggles with just these issues, especially when considering the downturn in economy in the 1980s, the higher divorce rates, and the absence of fathers in the home (Cherlin, 1988; Furstenberg, 1988), conditions that put masculinity in question in a similar way as masculinity was put in question in the periods Rotundo examines.

Had A Dad[xlviii]: Blankenhorn, Griswold and Mintz on Fatherhood

Blankenhorn (1995), Griswold (1993), and Mintz (1998) all trace the cultural construction of masculinity through the history of fatherhood. While Griswold (1993) and Mintz focus on the changing role and presence of the father, Blankenhorn (1995) instead focuses on the absence of the father, or fatherlessness.

Griswold (1993) traces the history and changes in fatherhood as tied to breadwinning and necessarily tied to shifts in the workplace and economy, yet also notes that this role as breadwinner removed men from the household and began an alienation of fathers and children, which defined American family life in the Twentieth Century (Griswold, 1993, p. 3). Further, Griswold observes that the rise in feminism over time has also placed demands of time spent with family onto the role of fathers (Griswold, 1993, p. 6; a similar idea is expressed in Mintz, 1998, p. 20).

The construction of fatherhood Griswold traces back to the 19th Century, when shifts in the family resulted in shifts in the construction of identity of children, that children we no longer "infant fiends" (Griswold, 1993, p. 11) but that they had personalities and needed attention, upbringing, and socialization. Around this time we see the training manuals, at first geared toward the father as emotional and moral head of household (Griswold, 1993; Mintz, 1998; Kimmel, 1996; Rotundo, 1993; Blankenhorn, 1995) and we see children's rooms as separate from adult bedrooms (Griswold, 1993; Mintz, 1998). Griswold notes that in upper class and landowning classes the introduction of servants freed the labor of the maternal parent, thereby allowing time for child-rearing as the shift in labor moved men's labor outside the home (Griswold, 1993, p.12; Mintz, p. 16). It is as though with the invention of leisure time, and the leisure class, we also have the invention of a parenting class, the invention of parenting time. Major shifts in the mode of production allowed for restructuring in the shape and structure and the ideology of the family.

Griswold reports of the late 19th/early 20th Century:

Rising numbers of men became commuters, shuttling between home and work. For those in the middle class, their destination might be an office in a bank or a place on the salesroom floor; for men of the working class, work might be in a small central shop or in a large factory. Regardless, urban and even town residents found that the bond once uniting men with their children had been broken. Increasing numbers of men now spent their days away from home, engaged in what became the defining characteristic of manhood for over a century – breadwinning (Griswold, 1993,pp. 13-14).

The effects of these changes were to dismantle the craft and guild structure of labor, so that fathers were no longer passing down a tradition of labor, heightening alienation of father and son, as well as worker and means of production, but also shaping men as earners and women as nurturers as the idealized forms of the differentiation in gender. Griswold (1993) also notes the legal shift resultant from the shift from men as emotional or moral heads of household in the legal shift, where fathers became legally the second parent, and culturally a secondary parent. Prior to this, Griswold notes (1993, p. 30), in contestations, children almost always automatically went with the father, however after the change in production children were generally awarded to the mother. Griswold (1993) and Blankenhorn (1995) make note of the film *Kramer vs Kramer* as significant in illustrating a shift in fatherhood in the 1980s wherein the father as nurturer is returned to.

Griswold and Mintz observe fatherhood to be tied to productivity, usefulness, and the economy as he suggests a "crisis" in masculinity, identified around the 1930s and 1940s as the depression and World War II removed jobs from men, or removed men from their country and thereby put the meaning of fatherhood into question as women moved in to fill their vacant roles. It is at this time, notes Griswold, that sexual identity scales appear on psychological tests, suggesting that the concerns of psychology are a reflection of larger societal concerns. Griswold quotes Joseph Pleck questioning: "What makes men less masculine than they should be, and what can be done about it?" (Griswold, 1993, p. 95).

With the shifts in the workplace defining masculinity, defining and differentiating masculinity from femininity, defining fathers from mothers, when that workplace is in jeopardy we see masculinity in crisis as brought on by the depression, as well as the fear of overly feminized boys raised by War Widows. We will note in Faludi (1999), later in this chapter, that the workplace may have been the last domain of men in the Twentieth

Century, and when that breaks down in the downsizing rightsizing Voodoo Reaganomics of the 1980s, men are left without identity, normless, anomic, and in deep crisis.

The War and the absence of fathers is where Blankenhorn (1995) picks up. Blankenhorn's central thesis is that fatherhood has been in peril since the Industrial Revolution, and that the post-war fatherlessness is different from pre-war in that fatherlessness is now voluntary, and he links this shifts in ideas of fatherhood that presents the role of the father as superfluous (Blankenhorn, 1995).

Two quotes from Blankenhorn are illustrative.

The United States is becoming an increasingly fatherless society. A generation ago, an American child could reasonably expect to grow up with his or her father. Today an American child can reasonably expect not to. Fatherlessness is now approaching a rough parity with fatherhood as a defining feature of American childhood (Blankenhorn, p. 1).

and

In 1990s, more than 36 percent of all children in the nation were living apart from their fathers – more than double the rate in 1960. The trend shows no sign of slowing down. Indeed, it seems quite probable that, as of 1994, fully 40 percent of all children did not live with their fathers. Scholars estimate that, before they reach age eighteen, more than half of all children in the nation will live apart from their fathers for at least a significant portion of their childhoods (Blankenhorn, p. 18).

Blankenhorn's tracing of the shifts in the construction of fatherhood vis a vis masculinity are similar to the previously presented work of Kimmel (1993), Rotundo (1993), and Griswold (1993), as well as Mintz (1998) Cherlin (1988), and Furstenberg (1988). Additionally, Blankenhorn attempts to draw a connection between fatherlessness and youth violence (Blankenhorn, pp. 26-28) as he surmises that the lack of role modeling is an issue. At one point in *Fatherless America,* Blankenhorn suggests the father to be the root of all society and civilization, bridging from Malinowski's *Sexual Life of Savages* in its search for the universality of the Oedipal Complex and the cross cultural

85

role of the father. The implicit point here is that with the breakdown of fatherhood comes the breakdown of society and social morality (Blankenhorn, p. 49).

Blankenhorn presents the statistics that almost a quarter of the American population was fatherless for two generations since World War II (Blankenhorn, p. 60), and cited the mother as central parent result as troubling to the masculine identity of boys. Further, Blankenhorn notes that the rise in feminism has resulted in the father-as-authority-figure coming into question as women become breadwinners, single, and sole parents, which he sees as eliminating, or at least giving short shrift to the role of the father, proposing the role of the father as "superfluous" in our current culture:

> More precisely, our elite culture has now fully incorporated into its prevailing family narrative the idea that fatherhood, as a distinctive social role for men, is either unnecessary or undesirable (Blankenhorn, p. 67).

Blankenhorn refers to television and cinema portrayals of fathers as illustrative of the transition from the stoic yet gentle and wise authority figure to the uninvolved, inept, or incapable father figure of more recent media, this is also supported by Mintz (1998) who notes *Married With Children's* Al Bundy and *The Simpsons'* Homer Simpson. Although this hardly constitutes direct and *scientific* evidence of Blankenhorn's observations, it will be remembered that the general thrust of this study entails popular culture as a reflection of the struggles, trials, and anxieties of the larger culture.

Blankenhorn's (1993) use of the Al Bundy and Homer Simpson father figures is further illustrative of the shift in fatherhood, from the detached breadwinner, once head of household, now something of an ineffectual figurehead. This figure of fatherhood is called into question and challenged as Blankenhorn cites the ideal for the "New Fatherhood" and the "like-a-mother-father", suggesting that the father be more nurturant, more sensitive, more understanding, more emotional, in short, more feminine (Blankenhorn, 1993). Mintz (1998) captures this notion of the shift in masculinity as embracing or encompassing attributes of the feminine as he cites *Tootsie, Mrs. Doubtfire, Mr. Mom,* and *Kramer vs Kramer,* as popular films of the 1980s, along with the *Cosby* television show, as portrayals that challenge, broaden, and expand the cultural construction of "traditional" masculinity to include and incorporate aspects of the feminine (Mintz, p. 21). In keeping with this project's central inquiry into the stereotypic attributes of the feminine in juxtaposition to hypermasculinity, it should be noted that the first two films mentioned had more to do in content with the visual or stylistic elements of the feminine, the outward appearance, or perhaps *drag* than they had to overtly to do with inward attitudes, beliefs, and behavior.

Despite the overt content of the above films, Blankenhorn, Griswold, and Mintz present a shift, a consolidation of the masculine and the feminine from the differentiation cited in Kimmel (1993) and Rotundo (1993) to the new conception of the more sensitive and emotionally engaged man. It is the position of this project that Metal Glam bears out the growing pains of this shift and consolidation.

Sweet Pain[xlix]: David Savran's Masochists, Martyrs, and Morrisons

In David Savran's 1998 work, *Taking It Like A Man: White Masculinity, Masochism, and Contemporary American Culture,* his basic thesis is that the construction of White masculinity has changed post-World War II, and this change results in a more *feminized* version of masculinity, characterized by masochism which represents a feminine position, perhaps suggestive of castration. No doubt this is a difficult thesis to digest in encapsulated form, yet Savran has followed the reasoning of all authors to present, until we hit the World War II era, at which point Savran observes the shift to suburbs and housing developments that were part of the post-War Veteran era, the outer lip of the Baby Boom and codification of White Middle Class America. The spirit of rebellion as a constant in American culture is also at the heart of Savran's (1998) thesis as he points to three cultural products to demonstrate a shift in the construction of masculinity: the Beat Movement of Burroughs, Keruoac, and Ginsberg (presented as occurring fresh on the heels of WWII in New York City); the film *The Wild Ones*; and the film *Easy Rider;* and implicates a fourth cultural product: Jim Morrison's self-imposed suffering, "sacrifice" and redemption as a new model of the Rock Star, which has its implications for Metal Glam and beyond: essentially these implications are for a new breed of misogyny wrapped in a more feminized package.

To begin at the beginning[l], Savran starts with the move to the suburbs, which decentralizes and de-unifies White men as a collective (Savran, 1998). Savran unpacks the trope of the White Man as a

87

generational construction, a product of its time: he positions pre-World War two White Manhood as identified with productivity, head of household, and staple of labor and economy (Savran, 1998). With the shift to post-War generations, White Manhood becomes decentralized and alienated from its status and power. For pre-War generations, trade unions, fraternal organizations, sporting associations, and other affiliations located in urban centers, identified along ethnic and racial lines, were rooted centers of "manness" and sources of identification of masculinity. Savran's formulation of history and culture follows that of Kimmel (1993) and Rotundo (1993). Yet, as the post-War housing push creates prefabricated suburbs and planned communities, this once center of manness becomes removed from the urban center. It literally becomes decentralized. The link to the trade unions, fraternal organizations, and other avenues of socialization and enculturalization become severed. Savran claims that this "fragmented the old solidarity and rechanneled aspirations" (Savran, 1998, p. 46). When considered with Griswold (1993) Blankenhorn (1993) and Mintz (1998), we have the picture of an increasingly alienated workforce concomitant with increasing alienation between father and son, changing expectations of the character of the masculine, and add the spirit of American rebellion into the mix and Savran portrays a youth movement searching for identity. Savran relies on Norman Mailer's icon of the "hipster", the disidentified youth who identifies with the downtrodden and marginalized. While this may have been a novel realization for Norman Mailer's time, we can plainly see this identification with the downtrodden in many youth movements: the identification with Black bluesmen in the R&B early 60s, the late 60s radicalism, Heavy Metal's "proud pariah" status as delineated by Weinstein (2000), Punk's self-generated post-modern rebellion ethos, and even at present in White audiences' identification with Hip-Hop and Rap icons.

Savran takes a long look at *The Wild Ones* as a cultural text reflecting the normlessness and search for identity inherited by America's youth (Savran, 1998). He also cites *Rebel Without A Cause* as depicting ineffectual father figures and rebellious self-marginalization in the search for identity and meaning (Savran, 1998). Within these films, also, is the *homosocial* bonding, the forging of solidarity through juvenile delinquency, reflecting the boy culture observed by Kimmel (1993) and Rotundo (1993) and enacted by Mötley Crüe, Poison, Ratt, Metallica, and countless other Heavy Metal and Metal Glam bands.

Savran present's Mailer's conceptualization of the White Hipster as the archetype of disaffected White Male Youth of the post-War generation. As the shift to the suburbs decentralizes the geography of masculinity and the identification of man-ness with trade unions and ethnic heritage via the fraternal lodges, the now-decentralized young men have been dis-identified in Savran's formulation. The dis-identified youth then identify with the outsider, the rebel without a cause, the White Hipster of Mailer. Savran hints at the transgression of formally held norms of identity and sexuality as he draws an analogy from the disaffected White Youth who "plays the part of the husband that scandalously desires to be like his wife, dress in her clothes, and co-opt her experience" (Savran, p.62) in the process of identifying with then outsider.

Further, the path to the Beat Generation and later Hippie counterculture is drawn by Savran:

> Embracing blackness, femininity, homosexuality, and poverty to declare himself white, masculine, heterosexual, and a man of independent means, he is unable, however, to stabilize any of these positions. In his confusion and multiplicity, he is the first exemplar of the postmodern subject who by the mid-1970s will become hegemonic in US culture (Savran, p. 52).

Savran demonstrates the confusion and search for identity through the emotive outpouring of Ginsberg's *Howl*, Kerouac's sensitive soul-searching and wanderings, and especially in Burrough's attempts to "master his femininity" as a man and as an artist (Savran, 1998). Savran focuses primarily on Burroughs as emblematic in the shift in masculinity following the war, the masculine as vulnerable rather than impenetrable, experiental rather than stoic, and emotive rather than controlled (Savran, 1998). With this, hypothesizes Savran, the Beats forged a new definition of male homosociality, a new definition of masculinity (Savran, p. 65). Part of this new definition included gender deviance in a self-identification and construction of anti-hero as hero.

The graphic homosexual acts and attitudes presented in Burroughs' novels seem to be significant in the reconstruction of masculinity to include *other-than-heterosexual*, but perhaps more significantly are the aspects of physical and mental suffering depicted in the works of Burroughs, of Swiftian proportion, yet significant and consistent with suffering depicted by his peers Ginsberg and Kerouac. In fact, the latter two Beats embraced Buddhism's central tenet that life itself is suffering.

It should be noted that it is not the contention of this study to propose that Burroughs, Ginsberg, and Kerouac were representative of their generation, nor should it follow that David Bowie, Alice Cooper or Nikki Sixx are representative of their respective generations. The point here is that Burroughs' *Naked Lunch,* Ginsberg's *Howl,* and Kerouac's *On The Road* were products of their time and place in American cultural history as much as Mötley Crüe and Poison were products of their time and place in American culture. Savran's point is that the Beat poets contributed to a reconstruction and reconfiguration of masculinity. We will examine how Metal Glam reconstructs and reconfigures masculinity to reflect its place in American culture and history in Chapter Five.

Back Off Bitch[li]: Susan Faludi and the Broken Promises of Post-War Masculinity

Susan Faludi's *Stiffed: The Betrayal of the American Man* (1999) presents portrait after portrait of men grappling with the decimation of the crumbling bastions of masculinity. She presents the Naval yards become ghostowns, a downsized defense industry, a Supreme Court-gender-integrated military school, as well as the social and interpersonal aftermath of World War II and Viet Nam veterans. As Faludi's (1999) journalistic tapestry of obsolete, unemployed and underemployed men, Lord-of-the-Flies cadets, and aimless adolescent Spur Posse members unfolds, she effectively traces a disintegration in the expectations of masculinity from post World War II to post Viet Nam.

Faludi, like Savran (1998) begins where Kimmel et al. leave off at post World War II. Her central thesis is that following the efforts of the Greatest Generation, White men were essentially promised the world, the moon, and the stars. She suggests this through the affordable housing and other benefits offered to WWII veterans (Faludi, 1999). Among these perks were government-sponsored jobs in the government-subsidized defense department (Faludi, 1999). As the recession of the 1980s hit, the defense industry was downsized, MacDonald Aerospace, reportedly a huge employer in the defense industry, merged with MacDonald Aerospace and eventually went belly up, leaving countless men in its wake (Faludi, 1999).

Faludi illustrates the plight of the unemployed man as a crisis in masculinity as one may infer that if, as Kimmel et al. suggest, the construction of masculinity is tied into man as worker, usefulness and productivity, and when employment is threatened, as Kimmel (1993) and Rotundo (1993) observe in their painting of trade unions as masculine solidarity, therefore the sense of masculinity is also threatened. Underscored in Faludi (1999) is the demise of the trade unions, which, given the above construction of masculinity via work, would produce a demise or threatening of masculinity itself.

As Faludi (1999) illustrates, more than the defense industry was hit by the recession of the 1980s, though: her recording of unemployed and underemployed men voice a sense of anomie, of uselessness, at odds with themselves, following the above suggestion of masculinity being threatened via employability and a man's place in the world as worker and breadwinner. Faludi's (1999) observations of the aftermath of the recession on masculinity notes domestic violence, substance abuse, sexual overcompensation, as well as conspiracy against the government. It would seem as though the promises made to men as inheriting the earth, as well as the premises of what it means to be a man are put into question post World War II. Perhaps the central question she poses is to the Greatest Generation who are asked by younger generations of men: "what have you done for me lately?"

In Mintz' (1998) work, he appears to echo or foreshadow Faludi:

> The perception that American men are in a sea of confused identities, emasculated egos, and misplaced priorities has elicited a wide variety of responses (Mintz, 1998, p 22).

Mintz (1998) talks about the Promise Keepers and Bly's Iron Johns, as does Faludi (1999) who presents these movements as men grappling with what masculinity means. Faludi's (1999) presentation of the Promise Keepers renewed faith in Christianity is painted as men reclaiming the position of emotional and moral head of household, as the previous authors cited in this chapter illustrate shifted to women as the nature and location of the workplace changed with industrialization. She similarly presents the West Coast Spur Posse, a loosely formed group of adolescents who gained notoriety for their competition of highest number of different sexual partners, which culminated in rape charges. Faludi's journalistic bent resists interpretation of the data, although the reader can connect hypersexual behavior with a quest to identify masculinity with sexual conquest, which becomes linked to the larger framing issue of *Stiffed* as

Faludi frames these teens as products of the failed aerospace industry as well as largely fatherless, which connects Faludi (1999) with Griswold (1993) and Blankenhorn (1995).

It is the portrayal of the cadets of the Citadel that is most chilling. Faludi (1999) follows the aftermath of the Supreme Court intervention at Charleston South Carolina's previously all-male military academy, the Citadel. Faludi (1999) reports not only the hazing and harassment of that institutions' first woman cadet, but also suggested racial and heterosexist-aimed hazing as well, as accounts and allegations of racially-motivated violence as well as homophobia are recounted by Faludi (1999).

Faludi's portrayal of the Citadel calls to mind William Golding's *Lord of the Flies*, a novel in which a group of boys are stranded on an island and revert to primative animality in the absence of any civilizing force, echoing the American social and cultural construction of a rougnh-and-tumble boyishness that avoids, evades, and eschews socialization and civility.

Aside from the William Golding overtones of the Citadel, what comes through Faludi's (1999) treatment of the Citadel is the defining of masculinity in contrast to the feminine, what Walser (1993) frames as exscription of women: the forging of masculinity through an exclusive solidarity. What is chilling about Faludi's (1999) illustration of the Citadel is that it goes beyond exscription and moves into the area of violence, becoming what Tipper Gore's Parents Music Resource Center feared about Heavy Metal.

The threat of violence paired with the exscription of women is important to note as Faludi's (1999) presentation of the Citadel suggests an extreme and violent reaction in a group of young men when their solidarity, when their identity as men, as masculine is threatened by the presence of women. A parallel may be drawn to unemployment similarly threatening men's sense of selves as workers and men, as Faludi (1999) presents narratives connecting the demise of the "working man" resulting in domestic violence. In both the traditional workplace, the factory, salesroom floor, the executive offices, and the military academy, the men-only code has been broached, and the line of reasoning that follows is that if work defines masculinity and work is threatened, then masculinity is threatened. Similarly, if enrollment and acceptance in the military academy identifies and defines masculinity, then when that is threatened, masculinity itself is questioned, for what makes a man a man if a woman can work the same job, hold the same position, and attend the same training program? Does masculinity then become defined by an active penis as the Spur Posse attempted? Does masculinity become defined by testosterone and aggression as the Citadel cadets and militia members attempted? Does masculinity become defined by usefulness, as one of Faludi's subjects found in jail, and found incarceration to be preferable to freedom because he could be useful (Faludi, 1999)?

As all of these crumbling bastions of masculinity once held a men-only rule, so did Heavy Metal in the 1970s and onward into the 1980s.

Girls, Girls, Girls[lii]: The Great Gender Divide in Heavy Metal

Heavy Metal became increasingly masculinized as it evolved from its roots of blues-inspired post-psychedelia. Walser (1993) and Weinstein's (2000) inclusion of biker culture in Heavy Metal's evolution organizes the emerging genre along lines of male bonding. Walser (1993) notes the origins of Heavy Metal, before the introduction of Biker culture, are found in the British art school background of the 1960s post-psychedelia/post-Yardbirds era, lending to exscription of women:

> The romantic ideology that was rampant in these schools stressed a bohemian ideal, which was both masculine and somewhat misogynistic (Walser, 1993, p. 102).

Walser also makes note of Michael Brake, who concludes that it Rock and Roll in general is "male dominated and predominantly heterosexual, thus celebrating masculinity and excluding girls to the periphery" (Walser, p. 103). So here we have Walser and Weinstein observing a gendered genre in Heavy Metal, founded in the heavily masculinized dominant form of Rock and Roll, and furthered in the hypermasculinized Heavy Metal, particularly in the themes of power, horror, and text and subtext in misogyny (Walser, 1993; Weinstein, 2000):

> Heavy metal musicians and fans have developed tactics for modeling male power and control within the context of a patriarchal culture, and metal's enactions of masculinity include varieties of misogyny as well as "exscription" of the feminine – that is, total denial of gender anxieties through the articulation of

fantastic worlds without women – supported by male, sometimes homoerotic[liii], bonding (Walser, 1993, p. 100).

In order to understand the exscription in the culture of Heavy Metal, it should be pointed out that prior to the formal genre codification of Heavy Metal (i.e., in the early 1970s, before Heavy Metal was a recognized genre term), formal gender differentiation in fan base may not have been as distinct as following the New Wave of British Heavy Metal. This may be due to the fact that Heavy Metal itself was not yet a crystalized and coherent genre and did not have a crystalized and coherent subcultural following. This is important in that as the genre develops and organizes itself, its sound, its themes, its values, it also organizes around gender lines. The "first wave" Heavy Metal bands such as Black Sabbath, the Blue Öyster Cult were still rooted in Rock and Roll and therefore any gender differentiation for these bands would have been close to the gender differentiation for Rock and Roll in general. As discussed above, other bands such as Aerosmith, Kiss, Alice Cooper, and Led Zeppelin were designated as "hard rock", a term more heterogeneous than Heavy Metal. Perhaps one might speculate that the lyrical themes of Black Sabbath appealed more to a male fan base than did the lyrical themes of Led Zeppelin, but a clear gender differentiation did not become apparent until the New Wave of British Heavy Metal, when Heavy Metal became almost exclusively masculine (Wasler, 1993; Weinstein, 2000).

Weinstein explains the gender differentiation in Heavy Metal as growing out from the late 1960s Hippie culture, a fusion of Woodstock and Altamont. Weinstein suggests that Heavy Metal's emphasis on power and aggression, socially constructed as attributes of masculinity, as a manner of reclaiming masculinity:

> …as the general youth culture, which was dominated by while males, fell apart, white, male, and heterosexual youth became socioculturally de-centered by emerging movements of women, gays, and non-whites (Walser, p. 101).

This ties in rather nicely with Savran's (1998) echoing of Mailer's White Hipster and Faludi's (1999) search for identity and the defining characteristics of masculinity in a landscape of shifting family structures, absent fathers, threatened work, new roles for women, and other perceived unfulfilled promises to the men that "should" have inherited the earth following World War II.

Further, the exscription of women in Heavy Metal and the exscription of women in places like the Citadel is very much along the lines of Robert Bly (1990) the Promise Keepers, and other forms of Men's Movements trying to figure out what masculinity is all about as masculinity has had not centrally organizing text in the way that Feminism has had a both a formal movement as well as a formal body of literature.

Terror n' Tinseltown[liv]: The Crisis in Masculinity

The "Crisis in Masculinity" appears to be renewed with each generation of young men facing maturity, concomitant with each set of changes in the social, cultural, historical and technological landscape. As this crisis shifts with each generation, it seems to be agreed that the decline of Western Civilization is a symptom of this elusive disease.

William Pollack's Real Boys (Pollack, 1998) documents the fact that our boys are in pain, they are in trouble, they are hurting. Our Boys, says Pollack, are straightjacketed within the "boy code"[lv].

Susan Faludi (1999) documents one example after another of the betrayal of the American Man, the post war era that has not kept its word to the men that inherit its earth. She asks the Greatest Generation what they have done for anyone lately.

David Savran's (1998) masochists, his Morrisonifications of the present era proliferate his pages as he attempts to explain the Timothy McVeigh's and other hurting white males who see themselves as victims.

We can read the crisis in masculinity into stories and popular culture productions: Kimmel (1993) paints the Wizard of Oz as an allegory of failing masculinity, citing the Tin Woodsman as a bereft industrialist, the Scarecrow as an impotent agriculturalist, and the Cowardly Lion as, well, a cowardly lion, a once-great head of state that is reduced to figure-head-mockery status. The use of *Wizard of Oz* as a masculinist allegory by Kimmel suggests that Frank L. Baum's narrative fiction of the 1920s and later the post-depression film respond to the tenor of their times and suggest crises in masculinity in both the 1920s and 1930s.

Kimmel (1993) also hints at the later 1970s-to-early 1980s Star Wars trilogy being the drama of Luke Skywalker's search for his father, one of Oedipal rebellion and identification. The late 1960s Star Trek is also mentioned as broadly painting the cold and unfeeling rationalist

95

masculinity juxtaposed to a passionate, muscular man of action in the guises of Mr. Spock and James Tiberius Kirk, respectively (Kimmel, 1993). Again, it may be drawn from Kimmel's observations that masculinity's crisis has been ongoing throughout the century, as reflected in the popular culture.

It should be noted that the "crisis in masculinity" is hardly a static crisis, but a dynamic one. The crisis does not stay the same and transmit from one generation of men to the next, but shifts and reconfigures as masculinity shifts and reconfigures with each generation. From the shift in economic organization from home-based work to industrial factory-based work, the role of men in the home shifted and the old definitions of what it meant to be a man were no longer valid in this new world of a new relation to the economy. Men needed to redefine their place in the workplace, in the family, in relation to women and in contrast to women. To flash forward in history, the increase in immigration to the United States threatened the previously established status quo of the White Male as dominant worker. A response to this was the revival of the guild model with trade unions and fraternal lodges, which sought to protect the role of men in the workplace, particularly White Men, and sought to make the world safe for future generations of Young White Men. The Boy Scouts, Christian Youth, and other youth groups that sought to "tame" and "civilize" the rowdyness and rough-and-tumble spirit of the boy also sought to socialize the boy into the future role of worker (Kimmel, 1993; Rotundo, 1993; Lowry, 1997).

In the history of masculinity we trace the decline of the patriarchy as the father is removed as emotional and economic head of household, and progressively removed from the home altogether. As the Women's Movement gathers strength in the 1970s the role of the father and the place of men is challenged further, to which there are two responses. One response is to redefine masculinity in a more rigid and "traditional" manner, in the style of Robery Bly's Hairy Men or Mötley Crüe's bad boys. The other response was to redefine masculinity in a less rigid and "traditional" manner and incorporate elements of the feminine.

As noted by Blankenhorn's (1995) observations of the "like-a-mother-father" and the new cultural requirements asking men to be more "feminine" in being more sensitive, emotionally expressive, and returning to the needs of family, this represents a shift, a consolidation of the masculine and the feminine. This shift of masculine and feminine combined appears culturally in the 1980s as noted by Mintz (1998) in his

96

citation of cultural products such as *Tootsie, Mr. Mom,* and *Mrs. Doubtfire.* This shift moves us from Kimmel's (1993) and Rotundo's (1993) definition of masculinity in the differentiation from the other. As we recall, this gender differentiation may be seen to be rooted in men's relation to the economy, technology, and the resultant changes in family structure. As we move into the 1980s, when the economy threatens men's sense of masculinity by challenging their previous status and their overall usefulness, as painfully detailed by Faludi (1999), and as demographics report the absence of fathers in the homes (Cherlin, 1998; Furstenberg, 1998; Griswold, 1993; Blankenhorn, 1995), raising fears of boys without manly guidance as paralleling Kimmel (1993), Rotundo (1993 and Mintz' (1998) observations about WWII-era boys growing up without fathers.

In short, while we see a pull to incorporate femininity into masculinity in the 1980s, we also see a push to strengthen the concept of masculinity by exscripting women altogether. We see this in Faludi's treatment of the Citadel (Faludi, 1999), in Robert Bly's Men's Movement, and in the homosocial aspect of Metal Glam and its larger cultures of Heavy Metal and Rock and Roll. It is the thesis of this project that Metal Glam illustrates the "growing pains" of masculinity redefining itself, that in its hypersexuality combined with stylistic elements of the feminine, the genre of Metal Glam attempts to negotiate incorporating femininity as well as excluding it altogether.

Examples of the heightening of masculinity as a construct in the 1980s are not hard to locate. Ronald Reagan projected a Teddy Rooseveltesque "rough and ready" presentation, recalling the cowboy mythos, perhaps intended to counterbalance his advanced age and stave off a public image as an infirmed elder, so masculinity and virility were projected, along with an unnatural shade of hair, although he would deny it being dyed. George Herbert Bush had his masculinity questioned as he fainted at a Japanese banquet, and bridled at being called a "wimp". One will also recall the indelible image of Massachusetts Governor Michael Dukakis in a tank, perhaps attempting to beef up his liberal image into an army of one.

Speaking of the army, G.I. Joe had his own cartoon on network television, and like the *Incredible Shrinking Man* cited by Faludi (1999), Kimmel (1993) and Rotundo (1993) as a cultural representation of masculinity in crisis, the size of the action figure shrank from 12 inches to less than half that size, although his face took on more of a snarl (as

97

opposed to the traditional stoic face with scarred cheek) and his weapons increased in size and deadliness.

In another platoon, Oliver Stone's films *Platoon*, and *Born on the Fourth of July* may have been grappling with post-Viet Nam veteran issues, but the 1980s also marked the return of the war film as a popular genre. One may argue that the war film never really died, only faded away, or became more complex, like Coppola's *Apocalypse Now*, or *The Deer Hunter*, but the introduction of Stallone's portrayal of Rambo marked the beginning of the 1980s, and Stallone continued to play this character throughout the decade.

Masculinity became buff and pumped as Arnold Schwartzenegger gained popularity and the expression "pumping iron" became lodged in the language. Children's cartoons of *He-Man, Master of the Universe*, sported the adventures of a hero who as so musclebound as to appear top-heavy, he was of course shirtless. Also in the 1980s professional wrestling came into the mass market with the likes of Hulk Hogan and others now largely forgotten.

It is indeed interesting to note that the suave and "genteel" masculinity of James Bond was more undercover in the 1980s while the unshaven and rough-edged *Lethal Weapon* Mel Gibson was granted cinematic license. As sexualized as Moore, Dalton, or Brosnin's James Bonds may have been, the 1980s seemed to move more in the direction of hairy and unruly Iron Johns rather than refined and genteel Remington Steeles.

As sex has been broached, it will be remembered that the start of the 1980s were regarded as years of casual and frequently anonymous sex before the outbreak of the AIDS virus. Television's *Three's Company,* and *WKRP in Cincinnati* appeared to be written around buxom actresses, and television characters were written as sexually active. One such character, Sam Malone, of the 11-season sitcom *Cheers* (played by Ted Danson, who, incidentally was originally not considered for the role as NBC was concerned he was not "masculine" enough) was portrayed as a gracefully aging lothario with overabundant libido. This was intended to be the strength of the character. Over the years, as the 1980s moved into the 1990s, the character of Sam Malone flirted with both marriage and monogamy, and eventually entered treatment for sexually compulsive behavior. The changes in this character are interesting to note as the construct of masculinity moved toward a more sensitive and emotionally expressive and available male.

As we noted the shift in culture alongside the shift in popular culture, our next chapter examines the shift in psychological culture as it attempts to wrestle with the elusive concept of masculinity and gender.

Chapter IV: A Review of the Psychological Literature

Chapter Three charted the social construction of the concept of masculinity alongside the shifts in numerous external forces such as technology, the economy, wars, and the rise of feminism. It was demonstrated that American cultural notions of masculinity were much entwined with these external factors and that as social and historical conditions shifted, so did concepts of masculinity.

While tracing the cultural context of masculinity in transition, the discipline of Psychology was not mentioned. This is not because Psychology does not have a parallel history of a cultural context for the concept of masculinity. In fact, it does. Griswold (1993) noted that during the 1930s, masculinity was a subject of concern to psychological researchers. Griswold does not go into detail about the nature of the inquiry, the construction of the research measures, or the assumptions underlying the research. This would have been of interest in placing the development of psychology as a field into the context of the social construction of masculinity.

In fact, it will be seen in this chapter that psychology as a field constructs gender and masculinity *as psychology itself is constructed by social and cultural forces throughout history*. Developments in psychology occur at specific points in history related to specific events and forces. As noted above, the field of Psychology is not separate from the social or cultural history from which it emerges. Much work has been done placing Freud, Charcot, Dora, Jung, James, and just about anybody who drew breath a hundred years ago into the social and cultural framework of the late 19th Century (Sulloway 1992; Foucault, 1973, 1980; Bernheimer and Kahane, 1985; Gay, 1988). This chapter will review the theoretical psychological literature pertinent to the construction of masculinity, femininity, and gender in order to present *this* history as running parallel to the histories of the social and cultural, as well as parallel to the histories of British Glam, Heavy Metal, and Metal Glam.

The ground covered in the forthcoming review of the literature of the psychological construction of masculinity will include empirical research, developmental theory informed by both psychodynamic and cognitive schools of thought, and Feminist psychological thought. It should be noted that this survey of the history of psychology is not meant to be exhaustive or comprehensive. Nor does this claim to be representative of the whole of the psychological field as numerous schools

100

of thought and movement are absent from this review (such as systems and family theories, neuropsychological research, physiological psychology [which has suggested biological contributions to gender and gender role, e.g. testosterone, etc.] and Lacanian schools of psychoanalytic theory, to name but a few). Instead, this body of literature has been selected as it highlights various turning points in the history of psychology that correlate with cultural and historic events in the social construction of masculinity as detailed in the previous chapter.

The centerpiece of our investigation will be the research of Anne Constantinople (1973) and Sandra Bem (Bem, Martyna, & Watson, 1976; Bem 1981, 1984, 1987a, 1987b), whose work in the exploration and conceptualization of the concepts of masculinity and femininity lead to a new definition of gender and gender role, which was seen to be independent of biology. The work of Constantinople and Bem refers back to earlier conceptualization of the constructs of masculine and feminine, and these will be touched upon in order to offer some backdrop.

Our next area of the literature will be culled from developmental theory, as both dynamic and cognitive schema models have conceptualized masculinity over time. We will also look at the later models and movements in psychology which occur after 1970, which will help keep our time-frame of 1980s Metal Glam in focus, as the theories and models that arise with Metal Glam may also reflect cultural constructs in transition. Here, we will briefly touch upon femininist theory and post-modern theories as movements within psychology that reflect external factors of a culture in transition.

If There's A Bustle in Your Hedgerow[lvi]: The Psychological Construction of Masculinity

As illustrated in Chapter Two, the year 1973 marked a high point in British Glam. This was a Rock and Roll whose hallmark was largely androgyny: the blurring and recombination of gender presentation and gender iconography. 1973 was also noted as a high point in for the founding fathers of Heavy Metal, with Black Sabbath and Led Zeppelin selling out stadiums, arenas, and festival venues. Unlike British Glam's stylistic norm of androgyny, Heavy Metal was masculinist and homosocial. For ten years these genres had little to do with one another.

1973 also marks a moment of transition in the psychological literature. This was the year Anne Constantinople published a paper reviewing the measurement of masculinity and femininity. In historical retrospect, Constantinople's paper suggested a turning of the tides in Psychology's construction and conceptualization of gender and gender role.

Got Your Mother In A Whirl, 'Cause She's Not Sure If You're a Boy or A Girl[lvii]*:* Masculinity, Femininity, and Psychological Androgyny

Constantinople's 1973 paper, *Masculinity-Femininity: An Exception to the Famous Dictum* (Constantinople, 1973) was the starting point in the re-examination of masculinity and femininity as *psychological* constructs as opposed to pre-existing, tangible, external *facts*. In this paper, Constantinople pulls apart the assumption of a psychologically inherent gender role by calling attention to the assumption that masculinity and femininity were previously conceived of as a single continuum. In other words, one was either "masculine" *or* one was "feminine". In her review of the history of gender role measurement, she calls attention to way the construct of masculinity-femininity is measured, and henceforth conceptualized.

Constantinople (1973) went back as far as Freud and Jung (as we will also when we get to the developmental models) in search of the roots of the psychological construct of the masculinity-femininity dimension. Yet, it was in the 1930s, as Griswold (1993) notes, that the measurement of masculinity became something to be concerned about by psychologists. As Griswold embeds this observation in a chapter on the Great Depression and the entry to WWII, we see a possible link between jobless fathers and absent fathers and the concern to quantify masculinity as historical events put masculinity into question.

Although Constantinople does not contextualize the psychological history of the masculine-feminine dimension, she only traces its development, she begins with the Terman and Miles study entitled *Sex and Personality* from 1936, the roots of the Strong *Vocational Interest Blank*, as well the roots of Hathaway and McKinley's *MMPI* in the 1950s (Constantinople, 1973). Constantinople notes that in the test construction, one is unable to distinguish whether these scales measure the respondent's espoused beliefs, "unconsciously" held beliefs, behavior, attitudes, or traits.

The distilled version of the Constantinople critique relevant to our work here is that the psychological construct of a masculinity-femininity scale was suggested to be rooted more in social convention and pre-existing behavioral norms than in independent differences between the

102

sexes. In illustration of this observation, we could look at the *present* MMPI-2 (Hathaway & McKinley, 1989) noted that a positive endorsement of careers traditionally associated with making, repairing, and activity are weighted on the masculine end of the Masculine-Feminine scale.

Constantinople's major critique of the "masculine-feminine" dimension is in the conceptualization of a single continuum, which she also notes has questionable construct and predictive validity (with the noted exception of determining the biological sex of the respondent). Instead, suggests Constantinople (1973) would it not be possible for one to have traits (beliefs, behaviors, ideas, etc.) which may be associated with *both* masculinity and femininity? This was the follow-up work of Sandra Bem (Bem, Martyna, & Watson, 1976; Bem 1981, 1984, 1987a, 1987b) and a host of other researchers. Bem (Bem, Martyna, & Watson, 1976; Bem 1981, 1984, 1987a, 1987b) is credited with proposing the idea of *psychological androgyny*, essentially the notion that an individual is able to combine both elements of feminine and masculine characteristics in order to achieve optimal functioning.

Bem's premise is that gender is a social construct (Bem 1981, 1984, 1987a/b) and becomes internalized by the individual. In her work, she cites studies in which the internalized notions of gender attribution are evident in schemata (ibid). As a social and cognitive construct, then, Bem challenges the "natural order" of "gender appropriate" behavior, values, interaction style, and identity and proposes that psychological androgyny "encourages individuals to embrace both the masculine and the feminine within themselves" (Bem, 1981, p. 362). Bem proclaims androgyny as a concept whose time had come (ibid), and cites as her purpose "to help free the human personality from the restricting prison of sex-role stereotyping and to develop a conception of mental health which is free from culturally imposed definitions of masculinity and femininity" (Bem, 1987a, p. 206). She further lauds the androgynous male as shunning "no behavior just because our culture happens to label it as female" (Bem, 1987a, p. 219).

Bem's proclamation of "better living through androgyny" has enjoyed some measure of empirical support. Stake et. al. (1996) examined "instrumental" (associated with masculine) and "expressive" (associated with feminine) characteristics, along with a social context variable, and their findings were that people with a balance (or, as in this, high in both) were also rated as higher in self-esteem, supporting Bem's (1974) hypothesis that "individuals who have a balance of 'masculine' and 'feminine' traits enjoy healthier psychological functioning than those who are stereotypically masculine or feminine." (Bem, 1974, as cited in Stake et.al., 1996, p. 167). The authors claimed: "Our results provide evidence of a positive association between perceived opportunities for androgynous functioning and self-concept and adjustment. Participants who reported high levels of both instrumentality and expressiveness also reported the highest self-esteem, well-being, relationship satisfaction, and self-perceptions of giftedness and likability" (Stake et. al., 1996, p. 184).

Green and Kenrick (1994) offer support for Bem's claim of psychological androgyny as healthy and optimal functioning in their study on heterosexual attraction and relational preference. Their results indicated that "both males and females express a preference for partners who exhibit both 'masculine' and 'feminine' characteristics" (Green and Kenrick, 1994, p. 252), although it was also noted that their women subjects valued androgyny higher than their male subjects.

Shaver et. al. (1996) found empirical support for Bem's idea of psychological androgyny as optimal functioning via attachment. Shaver et. al.'s research found that attachment security was related positively to both masculinity and femininity (via gender schema inventories) and hence to androgyny:

> Both attachment and androgyny are viewed as desirable, perhaps even optimal, mixtures of self-confident autonomy and healthy capacity for intimate, emotionally expressive relationships. The large literature on sex role orientations contains many indications that androgyny is associated with high self-esteem, romantic relationship satisfaction, less loneliness, better physical health, and desirable behavioral flexibility (Shaver, et. al. 1996, p. 583).

The idea of the possibility that masculinity and femininity could be combined to form a "psychologically beneficial amalgam, androgyny" (Shaver, et. al., 1996, p. 584), was not singular to the work of Bem. Spence (1984), along with Bem, questions the validity of concepts of masculine and feminine based on the empirical data, and sides with Bem on the notion of gender as socially constructed and transmitted. Spence also suggests that rather than a binary model or continuum, there are aspects of gender (masculinity and femininity) that may co-occur within the individual (Spence, 1984, p. 72). Spence, also, however, adds a developmental aspect to gender identity formation, suggesting that although "gender constancy" solidifies by the ages of four or five, "new developmental tasks may create stresses that cause individuals to doubt their masculinity or femininity and struggle to reaffirm it" (Spence, 1984, p. 84), and makes specific reference to gender affirmation tasks of adolescence (ibid).

Another element to the work of Spence was implications for social change and changing social norms, (Spence, 1984, p. 86). Spence referred to hippie long hair as non-conformity and rebellious, although also noted that in time this act of rebellion became co-opted by the larger culture and thus normalized (ibid). Here, the social construction aspect of gender schema and psychological androgyny are placed within historical context.

The historical context of Bem and Spence is picked up in Lorenzi-Cioldi's (1996) critique of the idea that androgyny transcends power differential in gender. Lorenzi-Cioldi makes reference to the historical and political climate of the 1970s, as well as images from popular culture including celebrities presented and lauded for transcendence of sex-role typing (androgynous). The author cites Morawski's notion that traditional prescriptions toward sex-role and gender identity were not so much discarded, but replaced by prescriptions for psychological androgyny, which amounted to a renovation rather than revolution. Lorenzi-Cioldi further argues that the psychologically androgynous personality ignores and therefore sustains social inequality between men and women (Lorenzi-Cioldi, 1996, p. 152).

Other critiques of Bem's proclamation may be found in Wilcove (1998), who examined perceptions of gender-schema in a both high school and college-aged gifted males, in a cognitive-developmental model. Although Wilcove suspended judgment about the generalizability of his findings, his results suggested that the young males in his study demonstrated some difficulty in fully integrating a pscyhologically androgynous self-concept. His findings spoke against a picture of masculine and feminine traits peacefully coexisting within the young male, despite intellectual acknowledgment of gender-role transcendence (Wilcove, 1998).

While gender role researchers Bem and Spence may have proposed combining elements of the masculine and the feminine as an ideal state, this ideal state may be difficult to realize. Lorenzi-Cioldi captures this difficulty in considering the relation of androgynous style to psychological androgyny as he cites Warren: "An androgynous appearance *may* be a sign of psychological androgyny, but it may also, as in the case of some rock stars, be a shallow veneer laid over a highly *macho* or male

105

supremacist character structure" (Warren, 1980, cited in Lorenzi-Cioldi, 1996, p. 142).

"Too Much %^#&@! Perspective"[lviii]: Making Sense of Sex Scale Literature
This observation is important to note, not only in that it captures the flavor of 1980s Metal Glam, but also because it brings to light the social and historical context that forms the backdrop to the psychological literature. No science, psychology included, operates in a vacuum that is untouched by the culture it is embedded within. It is interesting to note that Constantinople's groundbreaking 1973 critique historically follows on the heels of the Sexual Revolution, Women's Movement, as well as the birth of Post-Modern thought. Constantinople's paper bears the hallmark of Post-Modernism as she deconstructs a central cultural assumption about gender role: that one must be either/or. Constantinople's (1973) paper brought about a shifting in the psychological construction of gender, a dismantling of gender role, attitude, and belief that became "unhooked" from biology. This scholarly and scientifically rooted work very much reflected the changing social mores and norms following the Sexual Revolution, Women's Movement, and the wake of 1960s radicalism. We may also note that popular culture, in the guise of British Glam, was also "in tune" with the tenor of these times. Further, as Savran (1998) notes, cinema and literature, in the guise of 1969's *Easy Rider* and the post-Beat era was also moving away from a "traditional" view of masculinity and incorporating elements of femininity.

Bem's following work in the 1980s received positive empirical support, as suggested above. It should be remembered that the work of Bem and those who followed in support of the construct of a psychological androgyny (as a resolution to the binary mutually exclusive masculine feminine conceptualization of gender and gender role) were also, like Constantinople, following a social-normative ideological wave as much as they were engaging in empirical research. It is very interesting to note that the work produced in the early 1980s appeared to have more "cultural" steam coming off from the wave of 1970s gender remodeling and remaking, while in the later 1980s, as we see studies that suggest that attributes of masculinity, while they may not be the sole province of men, may be more desirable than psychological androgyny. The work of Powell and Butterfield (Powell & Butterfield, 1989) examined the concept of psychological androgyny in the workplace, and their findings suggested that masculinity was more adaptive to management. This is a very interesting finding when compared not only to Metal Glam's thrust of hypermasculinity as a result of masculinity in transition, but also when compared to Faludi's (1999) observations about the threat to masculinity in management in the late 1980s. In further illustration of the chronological change from a climate of psychological androgyny in transition to the attributes of a stereotyped masculinity, we also have the work of Marsh and Byrne (1991) who claimed masculinity to be more beneficial for the construct of self-concept, as well as an earlier piece by Lundy and Rosenberg (1987) finding similar claims, yet under the construct of self-esteem.

What is important here is not the answers but the questions. In other words, when the questions of psychological measurement change from "how masculine are you?" to "what is your balance of masculine *and* feminine traits?", this shift is important. The point here is that just as masculinity evolves, shifts, and transitions from one set of attributes to another that are tied very closely to historic-social-cultural forces, the same occurs in both popular culture and psychology. As the empirical researches into the construct of a masculinity-femininity dimension are but one segment in a larger whole of Psychology as a body of knowledge, we will turn our attention next to the developmental theories that have contributed to the construction of the concept of masculinity.

Youth Gone Wild[ix]: Developmental Theory

As noted in previous sections of this work, a comprehensive survey of the developmental literature would be both exhaustive and exhausting, therefore, the scope of developmental theory has been limited to, roughly speaking, two "camps" of the literature. With regard to our topic of investigation, masculinity in transition, we will therefore review the two developmental models that would help in understanding the construction of masculinity: conscious models and unconscious models. Hopefully this will satisfy those who conceive of develop as a cognitive-constructional process along the lines of Piaget, as well as those who conceive of development as a dynamic-experiential process, along the lines of Erikson.

Come In Here Dear Boy, Have a Cigar[x]: Dynamic Thought

The vast body of literature that addresses gender role and gender identity in the individual may be traced back to Freud's early theories of fundamental differences in gender. Freud's proclamation of "anatomy is destiny" was rooted in psychic organization, predicated on Superego development, rooted in castration anxiety (Freud, 1997/1924). Essentially, if one has a penis to lose, one has a healthy and functioning Superego to gain. The penis is equated with masculinity, and to be without a penis is to be equated with femininity. In psychoanalytic circles this essentialist position would later be further explored by Lacan (1982) and critiqued by Horney (1967).

Freud did, however, make note of a "masculine complex" in women (Freud, 1997/1924). Here is the idea that sexuality, or gender identity, is psychologically organized as a result of the passing of the Oedipal complex. Further, in a later work, Freud makes reference to the "bisexual" (or perhaps androgynous) attitude as an aspect of the emerging Oedipal complex (Freud, 1997/1925). The idea that Freud formally introduces a "bisexual attitude" suggests that his construction of gender is not binary (as a purely biological conception would be) and may instead represent a continuum, although implicit in his writing was the idea that gender identity must be consistent with biological disposition, else the gender identity becomes pathological.

Jung's conception of gender identity and its intrapsychic function combines both the binary and continuum models. Jung's model is one of conscious identification with one side of the binary model (either masculine or feminine), yet there is also an unconscious and complementary structure (Jung, 1977/1934). In other words, while one may consciously identify oneself as masculine, and while in such identification one may act and hold values that are "gender appropriate", the feminine aspects and values will be active in the unconscious (ibid). For Jung, it is not the "gender appropriateness" of character or attitudes, but more the balance of the complimentary forces, and the more one moves to the extreme in masculinity, for example, the more one's unconscious moves to the feminine ideal. Thus, in addition to combining the binary (in identification) and continuum (in the balance of complimentary forces), the idea emerges that the individual may have aspects of the masculine and the feminine without entering the realm of pathology. Pathology for Jung, was essentially an imbalance in complimentary forces. The idea of combining elements of both the masculine and the feminine for optimal functioning was explored in Jung's later work in archetypal psychology, where the figure of the androgyne was seen as the resolution of opposites, an ideal figure (Jung, 1980/1953,

1980/1959, 1983/1957, 1990/1959, 1989/1963). However, this bit of flexibility and forward thinking in Jung was never really absorbed into American culture until the 1970s, as we will later see in the upcoming section on post-1970 contributions. In the meanwhile, we will move forward to the thought of Erik Erikson, who took the Freudian model and charted a course for individual development. Following Erikson, we will then consider the contemporary dynamic thought of Peter Blos and Richard Lasky.

When I'm Enraged Or Hitting the Stage[lxi]: Erikson
    Erikson has been selected for inclusion in this study as the Eriksonian model of development has been a mainstay of dynamic psychological theory. In tracing the development of the personality from childhood to adulthood, Erikson lays out "normative", "expected", and "optimal" development, which, as will be seen in the section on Feminist Psychology, later is challenged as the assumptions of this normative model are the White Male. It is important to review the thought of Erikson as the theory lays out what is expected of men, and hence, contributes to the construction of masculinity.
    The work of Erik Erikson (1963, 1964, 1968, 1979) distills into an eight-stage model of development that enjoyed a good many years of dominance in dynamic and developmental psychology. Erikson retains the basic Freudian dynamic model of tension and satisfaction, but moves more with the Ego post-Freudian school than with the libinal or drive camps. Erikson's thrust as a theorist is to explain how the individual negotiates needs and environment and incorporates this into Ego, or as he frames it, Identity (Erikson, 1963; 1964; 1968; 1979).
    What is interesting to note about Erikson's developmental theory for our purposes is that many of the early (the pre-Identity) stages are heavily associated with the idea of masculinity in terms of the idea of man as a maker or a doer. Stages two through four have as successful resolution Autonomy, Industry, and Initiative, which culminate in Identity. This is interesting in light of the previous chapter's authors on the crisis in masculinity which note that when men's breadwinning is threatened, i.e., when industry, initiative, or autonomy are in jeopardy, then men's identity as men is also threatened. Faludi (1999) also portrayed how the crisis in masculinity could affect intimacy (as in the Spur Posse's consumer-oriented sex, or as in domestic violence seen in right-sized ex-aerospace managers or pre-Promisekeepers), generativity in the absent fathers

documented by both Faludi (1999), Griswold (1993) and Blankenhorn (1995). These authors, along with Savran (1998), Kimmel (1996) and Rotundo (1993) would also note that integrity, the final of Erikson's stages, is a particularly open wound in the crisis of masculinity.

As briefly noted above, Erikson's developmental model fits the crisis of masculinity rather well. In fact, Erikson's model becomes something of a blueprint for the construction of masculinity. Feminist critics such as Mary Ballou suggest that Erikson's model is primarily about male development as opposed to be being a unisex or gender-free developmental model (Ballou, 1992). The heart of this criticism is that the Eriksonian reliance on independence as opposed to interdependence and individuation as opposed to being-in-relation betrays the tenor of post war (WWII) dynamic theory being based on the norm of masculinity, following the lead of Freud's early theory of the necessity of the penis for the possession of a Superego.

With the benefit of 21st Century hindsight, it would appear as though Erikson's developmental model, which, it will be reminded to the reader, was the dominant model for development for a significant period of time in American culture, was not only based around the male as the norm, but also the assumptions of the ideal of American masculinity as seen in the stresses on independence, individuation, autonomy, activity, and strength[lxii]. This singular strong-willed figure, reflecting the ideals of American culture, may be seen in cultural archetypes such as Teddy Roosevelt's Rough Rider period, John Wayne, even the Marlboro Man. These characters are expected to stand on their own, stand up for themselves, be silent and strong, and ride into the sunset without complaining. The dark side of this image comes through in characters such as the brooding Batman, Clint Eastwood's world-weary weapon wielding wayfarer, the Man With No Name, and Stallone's Rambo (although as all of these characters have issues with Basic Trust, they may not be considered to Eriksonian heroes per se). Pollack, in *Real Boys* (1998) considered this "boy code" of silence and stoicism to be a problem in the emotional development of boys, yet he only criticizes our culture, not the developmental model. It would seem that as Erikson's model is no longer held as the coin of realm for development, that this reflects also a transition in our culture, picked up by Pollack, that we no longer expect our boys to be silent sufferers.

110

"Mom and Dad Are Rolling On the Couch, Rolling Numbers, Rock and Rolling, Got My Kiss Records Out[lxiii]*"*: Blos and Lasky

More recent dynamic models of development shift from an Ego focus to an Object focus, referring to unconscious and internalized parental/experiential figures or objects that speak to a more relationally oriented psychology. This very shift itself is interesting historically, that as we move from the post WWII ideal of masculinity as an individual, independent, and industrious man, we move to a new ideal of masculinity as interdependent, related, and nurturing as noted in Blankenhorn (1993). Reflecting this is the organization of our dynamic theory, which moves from a one-person, Ego-focused theory to a two-person, relationally oriented theory.

Peter Blos, who emphasizes the contribution of drive (Blos, 1962, 1979), frames adolescence in a Kleinian manner as a recapitulation of early childhood [Klein 19xx] and focuses on a reawakening of preOedipal organization as well as Oedipal material. Blos looks particularly at the twin drives of libido and aggression in the adolescent male. This works very nicely with the rebellious content and attitude of Heavy Metal as a re-awakened Oedipal complex, in which the adolescent male identifies with a phallocentric Heavy Metal, complete with masturbatory imagery of long-drawn-out guitar *solos*. This rebellious Heavy Metal, which contains an angry and rebellious lyrical content, is perhaps directed toward father-figure authority figures, although there is no *perhaps* in the early 1980s videos of Twisted Sister which pit the adolescent male against the father in a revelry of cartoonish violence.

Blos even conceives of an unresolved or negative outcome of the Oedipal complex in the male child's failure to identify with the father (Blos, 1979, p.27). This "negative Oedipal complex" figures in the foreground as Blos ponders the problem of teen violence in the late 1970s resulting from absent fathers or fathers who failed to present as role models to be identified with. As suggested previously, this psychological conceptualization reflects the tenor of its times: Blos' 1979 *The Adolescent Passage* remarks on a cultural *anomie*, a societal breakdown as illustrated by youth violence and youth aggression seen in anti-Vietnam protests, college riots, and other unidentified social ills following the waning of the Summer of Love. Blos conceives of the turmoil of the late 1960s/early 1970s as the outgrowth of the "negative Oedipal" outcome. Further, this conception suggests a growing discontent in young men, perhaps suggesting a crisis in masculinity as the father is not identified with and thus young men are affected by this poor Oedipal outcome. Blos continues to speculate that in the adolescent male's seeking gratification from a parental figure, he is confronted with "a hovering castration anxiety", presumably the outcome of poorly developed Superego, resulting from poorly negotiated Oedipal resolution (Blos, 1979).

Blos appears to paint something of a bleak picture for young men, quite different from the map of development laid out by Erikson for the pre-World War II boy. It seems almost as though Blos represents the midway station between Erikson's masculine ideal of yesterday and Pollack's silent sufferer of today.

Blos' dynamically oriented twin drive theory of libido and aggression (it will be remembered that the original Freudian model suggested these as Eros and Thanatos (Freud, 1959/1920), and this was among the sources of the break with Jung, who felt that a de-eroticized libido could become aggression as he conceived of libido as a "life force" [Jung, 1980, 1990]), could also speak to our central problem concerning a hypermasculine aggression in the trappings of sexualized feminine attire. Under Blos' elaboration of the Freudian notion of the twin drives of libido and aggression, we may take the presentation of the Metal Glam style as a symbolic representation of the aggressive drive and the libidinal drive in the guise of platform shoes, lipstick and mascara: i.e., the Metal Glam performer become the object of libidinal drive while simultaneously engaging in aggressive drive. This interpretation would also work nicely with the analytic dictum that there are no negatives in the unconscious and that this seeming clash in sexualized elements would be understood as something of a compromise.

As Blos deals with the father, so Lasky emphasizes the mother. Lasky (1993) follows Blos' lead in framing adolescence in the Kleinian mode of a recapitulated early childhood. But in focusing on the adolescent males' preOedipal experience with the mother, Lasky moves away from the threat of castration and instead focuses on the loss of mother.

Lasky, among other contemporary dynamically-oriented developmental theorists, regards the task of adolescence as separation and individuation. This is very rooted in Eriksonian thought, perhaps as Erikson was very rooted in dynamic thought as well as seeking to assimilate into the larger culture of America. Lasky feels that the object, meaning the mother, must be renunciated in adolescence (Lasky, 1993, p. 105). Presumably, for this individuation and separation to occur, the adolescent male would need the internal resources of an internalized maternal imago, an internalized object.

So, to look at Metal Glam from the Lasky-loss-of-mother-in-adolescence perspective is to take another look at the makeup and mascara. Rather than the object of libido expressed in the teased hair and defined cheekbones of the Metal Glam icon, this feminized appearance has more to do with the loss of the maternal figure while asserting separation in the act of rebellion.

This application of Lasky's theory of time-honored normative male adolescent development works nicely with the new ideal of a "softened" masculinity (or the *like-a-mother-father* as Blankenhorn (1995) terms it) as more in touch with femininity. In other words, to compensate for the loss of mother, femininity becomes incorporated into masculinity. However, Lasky's theory does not adequately explain the hypermasculine element in Metal Glam of the 1980s. In that Lasky was published in 1993, this suggests that his theory would be more contemporary with the tenor of the post 1980 world, and would not necessarily speak well to the phenomenon of Metal Glam as that was a period which had passed. In fact, Lasky's focus on the loss of the mother-object actually fits better with the themes of Grunge and Industrial of the early 1990s, in which masculinity was painted as openly suffering and vulnerable as noted in Savran's (1998) study on masculinity in transition.

Throughout this literary history tour of dynamically oriented developmental theory, we note that the prescribed notions of the masculine ideal for each age appears to be very rooted in the culture of its time. From Freud's early notions of masculinity rooted in male biology, to Erikson-informed image of the pre-World War II American Marlboro Man, to Blos' angry young men to Lasky's current young man who grapples with the loss of mother, the dynamic developmental models appear to shift along with the larger culture's shifting images and definitions of masculinity.

The Mind Is A Terrible Thing To Taste[lxiv]: The Cognitive Developmental Theories

As hinted at above, the conceptual corollary of a dynamic or unconsciously-rooted developmental model is a developmental model rooted in conscious mentation, or, in plain English, a cognitive developmental model. The cognitive model to have held court in developmental psychology for a number of generations of psychologists

113

has been that of Jean Piaget. To summarize the thrust of Piaget's work succinctly would be to say that Piaget frames development as a task of building cognitive schema (Piaget, 1926, 1954, 1958; Ginsburg & Opper, 1988). The child begins to develop mental maps of how the world works which become increasingly complex and increasingly flexible as the child moves from one stage of intellectual development to the next.

The Piagettian model becomes applicable via the work of Bem and those who followed her lead into the idea that androgyny represented the wave of the future. Bem conceived of psychological androgyny as a more adaptive and more developed cognitive schema that allowed for the incorporation of both the masculine and the feminine attributes of gender (Bem, Martyna, & Watson, 1976; Bem 1981, 1984, 1987a, 1987b). Bem often referred to the term "gender schema" (Bem, Martyna, & Watson, 1976; Bem 1981, 1984, 1987a, 1987b), which owes its conception to the Piagettian system of stages of cognitive schema. The important aspect of the influence of the Piagettian developmental model on the research on psychological androgyny and gender schema is that this model is a *cognitive*, i.e., conscious model, and therefore stands separate from a dynamic model which places emphasis on unconscious and dynamic structures. We will also later see the influence of the Piagettian model on Kegan's conceptualization of development in terms of a developmental model based on cognition and meaning making.

Another cognitive model to gain dominance in the field of Psychology was Kohlberg's theory of moral development (Kohlberg, 1984). Kohlberg's gist is that the individual's intellectual development moves from and egocentric self-preservation focus to a broader and wider perspective which may entertain lofty idealistic notions such as "morality", "justice", and something akin to Socrates' conception of "the good". Within this cognitive developmental framework, Kohlberg has also applied his ideas to gender identity and gender role development. Essentially, Kohlberg proposes that the individual's identification of gender and gender role are areas of cognitive development that begin with what he coins as "gender constancy" at roughly the age of four or five (Kohlberg, 1966, 1969; Kohlberg & Zeigler, 1967).

While this may be an interesting notion to see in print, the skeptical (read jaded) reader cannot help but compare this idea to Freud's notion of Superego development around the age of four or five (which is the result of identification with the father, for boys, which would be another way to say "gender constancy"), or comparing it to Piagettian

Concrete Operations (at roughly this age and stage), or even dipping into a neuropsychological timetable which places a more sophisticated language development at the age of four or five which would suggest that such "constancy" is not isolated to gender, but the ability to linguistically encode and retrieve data via developing temporal lobe structures.

The contribution that Kohlberg does make, however, is that within this process of "gender constancy" is the learning, or socialization of gender-typed (or gender stereotyped) roles and behavior (Kohlberg, 1966, 1969; Kohlberg & Zeigler, 1967). This suggests, along the lines of Bem (et. al) that at an early age the child learns not only of gender, but of behavior, attitudes, and attributes of gender. Kohlberg's ideas become applicable to our object of inquiry as Leahy and Eiter (Leahy & Eiter, 1980) explore the adaptive benefits of psychological androgyny under the framework of Kohlberg's "post-conventional" stage of moral development. Post-conventional moral development essentially refers to the individual who is able to, as the title implies, apply reasoning and problem-solving skills that move beyond conventional reason and social morays. This would be akin to "thinking outside the box" along the lines of Nietzsche who challenged the conventional norms of morality.

Leahy and Eiter conceptualize an individual's adoption of attributes of both masculine and feminine traits, behavior, and attitudes to fit within Kohlberg's higher stages of cognitive-moral development, especially as adpativity and flexibility are noted in moving outside of a rigid gender-bound framework.

In this light we may view our object of inquiry, the clash of hypermasculinity with stereotypic elements of the feminine, as perhaps "growing pains" in cognitive-moral development, that as there *is* a clash of elements, e.g. misogyny in mascara, this represents a state of developmental tension, perhaps not unlike the tension Piaget speaks of between stages (Piaget, 1926, 1954, 1958; Ginsburg & Opper, 1988). It is speculated here that the cognitive tension experienced between stages of Piagettian development is expressed outwardly in the tension between stylistic elements of the feminine and the masculine. This may be a way of conceptualizing our central question along cognitive developmental lines.

From Piaget and Kohlberg, we now come to Robert Kegan, whose theory has become *development du jour*. In reading Kegan (1982), one rapidly becomes aware of the influence of Piaget and Kohlberg in Kegan's emphasis on cognitive development, yet there is also a dimension of dynamic flavoring in the notions of attachment and Eriksonian Ego development that are embedded in Kegan's rhetoric. The highlighted concepts in Kegan's synthetic blend is the developmental task of balancing differentiation and inclusion (Kegan, 1982). Key words in the Kegan system are *growth, balance,* and *loss.*

In discussing adolescence, Kegan notes that the parental figures are the objects of differentiation and inclusion, and this is how he frames the adolescent task of breaking away from parents yet maintaining relatedness. When we apply this to our central concern of Metal Glam, we may understand the clash in tropes as another form of "growing pains" in that the clash of elements represents difficulty in balancing individual and institutional, i.e. the individual conceptions of self and gender role with the societal and cultural norms which prescribe gender-typing.

Heads Explode[lxv]: Making Sense of the Cognitive Developmental Model

As attempts have been made to explicate and illustrate while delineating the major models of cognitive developmental theory, it will suffice here to summarize as follows: the cognitive developmental models focus on the building and expanding of mental maps, and in moving from an embedded egocentrism to a perspective that is able to step outside of the immediacy of a constructed self. In plain English, the contributions of the cognitive developmental theories are that gender identity and gender role may be "unhooked" from biology and seen as social constructions or social conventions rather than as absolute or imperative.

Cognitive developmental theory posits that the individual may become able to step outside of their own personal egocentrism, either in Kohlberg's postconventional stage or Piaget's move beyond concrete operations. It follows then, that other aspects of the self, such as gender role, may be moved beyond in a fashion similar to egocentrism: just as one realizes that one's perspective is not the only one, or as one realizes that rules and norms are cultural constructions, one may also realize that gender and role may be synthetic products of a time and culture rather than "natural" attributes of a self.

My Brother's Back at Home With His Beatles and His Stones[lxvi]: Psychology in the Post-1970s

Just as Chapter Three placed the cultural construction of the concept of masculinity into an historical framework, so we must do the same for the field of Psychology as we review the pertinent literature. It should be noted that each of the previously mentioned schools of thought had their formative periods in the early part of the 20th Century: the dynamic developmental model is rooted in the Freudian tradition of the dawn of the 20th Century; Piaget's theory goes back to the 1920s or thereabouts; and even though Constantinople marks a transition in 1973, her work was referring back to the psychological measurement of the masculine-feminine dimension going back to the 1930s.

The point here is that the 1970s mark a significant transition phase which we note culturally in the Sexual Revolution and the Women's Movement, which had significant impact on the cultural re-definition of masculinity. Further, the 1970s mark the development of British Glam as well as Heavy Metal as genres underpinning the object of our study, Metal Glam. Furstenberg (1998) observes the 1970s as marking a major shift in demographics concerning the American family, namely the absence of fathers[lxvii], as does Blankenhorn (1993) and Griswold (1993). Again, all this sets the stage for the social, cultural, familial, and political atmosphere of the 1980s, which frames the backdrop of Metal Glam and its hypermasculine adnrogynes.

In that the historical advances of the 1970s are seen to be important to our investigation, we will next examine three areas of psychological thought that developed in the intellectual landslide of 1970s Psychology. We will look at the contribution of Feminist Psychology, we will look at the Jungian Revival, and we will also look at Judith Butler's notion of gender as performance, resulting from Gender Theory, an outgrowth of Feminist Theory. It should be noted that these reviews are not intended to be exhaustive or inclusive of the whole of a school of thought, but mere thumbnail sketches as they apply to the object of our inquiry.

Girls Rock Your Boys[lxviii]: Feminist Theory Makes Its Entrance

The Women's Movement, following on the shrinking high heels of both the Sexual Revolution of the late 1960s/early 1970s and the Civil Rights Movement of the late 1950s/early 1960s was undoubtedly the cultural impetus to the evolution of a Feminist Psychology emerging in the late 1970s/early 1980s. Landmark authors such as Gilligan (1982) and Chodorow (1989) follow on the previous thought of Horney (1967), Deustsch (1944) and de Beauvoir (1968) to begin to articulate a psychology that does not hold as its unspoken norm the White Male Experience.

117

It should be noted that these criticisms have been met by history as the field of psychology has shifted from a male dominated to predominantly female dominated. The percentage of female graduate students in psychology has grown over the past twenty to thirty years to the point that men comprise less than half, perhaps only as much as ten percent of graduate psychology students[lxix]. Currently, the norm of the White Male Experience is indeed being challenged by psychology.

Feminist Theory challenges the previously prevailing norms of psychological theory that were seen to be based in a bias of male developmental norms (Gilligan, 1982; Chodorow, 1989). The contribution that is relevant to our investigation here is that the emerging school of Feminist Psychology was seen to support a less gender-bounded notion of "normal" development. This may be seen to have influenced, in theory at least, Constantinople's inquiry into the psychological construction of the masculine-feminine dimension, previously unchallenged.

Just as the Women's Movement and Feminism began to challenge the previously prevailing dominance of Patriarchy, so did Feminist Psychology begin to call attention the assumptions inherent in the then-prevailing masculine-based Psychology. The advent of Feminist Psychology allowed for a re-working of the psychology of women just as the Women's Movement allowed for a re-working of the role of women in American culture. The challenging of biologically-bounded notions of gender identity and gender role became less pathologized after the advent of Feminist Psychology as seen in the Bem (et. al.) flurry of research which sought to prove the benefits of incorporating aspects of both masculinity and femininity.

As Feminist Psychology deconstructs the "feminine psychology", it reveals the "masculine psychology" which had been previously unexamined and buried under the rubric of "the norm". Just as Feminist Psychology uncovered masculine psychology in its uncovering of feminine psychology, previously unexamined, unnamed areas of heterosexual, White, and Middle Class were revealed as well (Frankenberg, 1993).

The rise of Feminism and Feminist Psychology may be seen as the necessary precondition to the re-examination of masculinity in the 1980s. This may not only be seen in the Robert Bly (1990) mytho-poeic explorations of masculinity, but also in the popular press, exemplified by such works as Real's *I Don't Want to Talk About It* (Real, 1997), and Pollack's (1998) *Real Boys.* Both these works sought to re-examine masculinity and attempted to make a case for an inclusionary model

118

incorporating elements of both the masculine as well as the feminine. In this context, the observer may be tempted to frame Metal Glam as an effort to incorporate both elements of the masculine and the feminine in a stagey, stylistic, rebellious manner (as befitting the culture of Rock and Roll), although the pieces simply do not fit. There is too much of a clash in tropes as the stereotypic cosmetics appear to parodize feminity rather than represent any of the integral aspects of attributes of the feminine. Especially as lyric content and visual presentation of Metal Glam icons of Motley Crue have more in common with Kubrick's rendering of *Clockwork Organge* than with Bem's promise of better living through androgyny. In this manner, the Metal Glam icon becomes more *androogynous* than androgynous.

Music From the Elder[lxx]*:* The Jungian Revival

Jung became part of the college curriculum in the 1970s and 1980s in the Northeast and West Coasts, at least[lxxi]. Often, the inclusion of Jung would be under the auspices of the English Department, but just as often, Jung would find his way into freshmen Psychology survey classes as dynamic theories of personality are outlined. Perhaps as Feminism, the Sexual Revolution, and the Anti-War Movements all sought to overturn the previously existing conventions of American Culture, the previously existing norm of a Freudian-oriented Psychoanalytic theory was also being challenged in the 1970s and 1980s. As Feminist Theory and the new waves of Cognitive Behavioral Theory rose in challenge to a perceived Freudian patriarchy, perhaps interest was re-awakened in Jung as a challenge to a Freudian status quo.

In any event, we see the influence of Jung working his way into the popular culture by the 1980s. During an episode of the NBC sitcom *Cheers* (located in the early to mid-1980s, ending in 1992), Shelly Long's character Diane Chambers makes a reference to Jung as an example of her character as intellectual, erudite, and *hip*. Beyond the world of sitcom we have the *graphic novels* (i.e. comic books) of the 1980s, most notably *Arkham Asylum* (Morrison, 1989) which clearly uses Jungian archetypes as the Shadow and features Batman's inward journey into darkness complete with chthonic challengers, Jung actually appears as a character in the narrative. Also in the mid 1980s was the popular band The Police's *Synchronicity* album, on whose cover Sting can be seen reading a Jung book, while the album title itself references Jung.

As part of this Jungian revival is the work of June Singer, who began compiling notes for a book titled *Androgyny: The Opposites Within* (Singer, 1997/1976). It is interesting that this book was first published in 1976, very close chronologically to Constantinople's 1973 critique on the psychological construct of a masculine-feminine dimension. It would seem that Singer's contemplation of our inner processes with regard to gender were part of the cultural fabric of challenging the previously held norms in the 1970s.

Singer's exploration of the archetypal representations of androgyny follows a Jungian line of thought: that the "journey" of one's development is a process of individuation, that one evolves or grows as a resolution of opposites. Jung's quarternity model of two poles of opposites that must be integrated for the healthy or successful person (psychologically, that is) is examined by Singer as including gender among the poles of opposites within (Singer, 1997/1976).

Without much bending, one could fit the Constantinople and Bem (et. al) of better living through androgyny, i.e., the individual's incorporation of both aspects of the feminine and the masculine as adaptive and representing a higher-functioning individual, into a Jungian or Singerian paradigm of union of opposites of masculine and feminine. We may, in fact, look upon the phenomenon of Metal Glam in the 1980s as a cultural expression of the press for a union of opposing forces of masculinity and femininity within the person of the Metal Glam icon. In other words, we may look upon the clash of elements of hypermasculinity and stylistic attributes of the feminine as a culturally unconscious symbolic expression of a need to integrate the masculine and the feminine for our culture to progress to a new level of *wholeness.*

In this light we may consider the Metal Glam icon to be a resolution of the opposites within our culture, expressed as a resolution of opposites within an individual. Despite the meta-metapsychological appeal such a reading of Metal Glam may hold, the homosocial elements of Metal Glam combined with the misogynistic lyrics and sexually exploitive behavior of the Metal Glam icons suggest that such a Jungian reading might have been more appropriate to British Glam of the 1970s than to American Metal Glam, which appears more like domination than resolution. Both Weisntein (2000) and Walser (1993) point out the misogynist culture of Metal Glam which served not only to objectify women but to exscript women, writing them out of the narrative except as trophy or threat. Both Walser (1993) and Weinstein (2000) note that this was also the fate of women who attempted to turn tables and become the Metal Glam performers: in addition to being largely ignored, they were generally only noticed for non-musical attributes, such as hair and wardrobe (or lack thereof), reigniting an old double-standard in American culture.

In short, had misogyny and exscription of women not been an integral part of Metal Glam, the Jungian/Singerian resolution of opposites toward a cultural wholeness might make a nice theory.

First Comes Pancake Batter Number One[lxxii]: Judith Butler and Gender as Performance

Just as Jung's influence may have been more heavily felt in the English Department rather than Psychology, so too may Postmodern Feminist Theory have more cultural currency in the Philosophy and Women's Studies Departments than among assigned reading for APA interns[lxxiii]. In the interest of brevity, Postmodern Feminist Theory essentially follows Michel Foucault's (1990/1976) line of reasoning that there is a dominant discourse which maintains the structure of power within culture. Postmodern Feminist Theory takes the critical position of Foucault a step further to claim that the dominant cultural discourse is one of a masculine heterosexual matrix, which becomes the normative standard of Culture. Enter Judith Butler and her 1990 work *Gender Trouble*, which critiques the notions of a "fixed" gender and gender identity.

As Butler looks at the problems of essentialism and *gendering*, her central claim is that one does not *have* a gender so much as one *acts* or *performs* a gender. In her Preface she refers to Drag actor Devine (of numerous John Waters films) and links the performance of gender in *drag* as a link to the performance of gender in general. Further, Butler notes, that the performance of drag itself destabilizes the notions of a fixed gender (Butler, 1990, p. xi) and calls attention to performance aspects of gender as a whole.

It is the notion of performance that has a special impact with regard to our central problem of the presentation of Metal Glam. We will also note the notion of a destabilized gender as revealed in the performance of drag as we tweak the Postmodern Feminist Theory to suggest that Metal Glam does not attempt to *pass* in an Erving Goffman manner. The Metal Glam icons do not try to appear *as* women, but in their makeup, spandex, platforms, and teased hair, they are parodying the stereotyped attributes of femininity as much as Butler's read on Devine.

121

Where the tweak in Butler's theory comes in is the proposal here that Metal Glam does not attempt to destabilize gender in its parodic performance, but that the presentation of Metal Glam may be read as symptomatic of a *gender that has been destabilized.*

As we observed in our cultural chronology in Chapter Three, the cultural concept of masculinity has been in flux throughout civilization: the idea of what it means to be masculine, what it means to be a man, the manner in which a man can identify himself as such in either differentiation to another or in description to himself, has never been stable. In short, the very notion of masculinity has always been "under construction", yet perhaps the most destabilizing movements occurred during the 1970s, the Women's Movement, the Sexual Revolution, and the generation landslide that called into question previously held norms and mores of social meaning making. The generation of the 1980s then, as illustrated by Faludi (1999), Griswold (1993), and Blankenhorn (1995) felt the aftermath of these shifts, among them a destabilized notion of masculinity. As shall be illustrated in the next and last chapter, Metal Glam was a particularly American cultural response to particular shifts in the norms and meaning making in American culture.

Chapter V: Conclusion

The last chapter ended on a note of a destabilized masculinity in American culture to which Metal Glam becomes a response from the collective consciousness of Pop Culture that seeks to restabilize masculinity. Bound up in the seemingly innocuous appearance of bands such as Twisted Sister, Mötley Crüe, and Poison, is not only the chance meetings of Heavy Metal and British Glam, but an American musical movement which appears linked to the shifting gender roles and identities of American masculinity and femininity.

One More Time[lxxiv]: Review and Recap
As noted in the previous chapter, the Post-War (WWII) era in the field of psychology is marked by shifts and revolutions of understanding. The once long held notions of "normative development" were examined in a different light, in different voices by the emerging Feminist Psychology, and subsequently challenged. In so doing, "feminine psychology" became differentiated from the previous conception of "psychology", and in the parsing out of the feminine necessarily differentiated a "masculine" psychology. Both the Chodorows and Gilligans, as well as the Pollacks and Reals posed the same question in the 1980s: what does it mean to be a man and what does it mean to be a woman in our time.

It is interesting to note that the differentiation and quest for meaning in gender followed an "unhooking" of gender from biology as well as a dismantling of the binaries of gender in the work of Constantinople (1973) and Bem (Bem, Martyna, & Watson, 1976; Bem 1981, 1984, 1987a, 1987b). In other words, as the empirical researchers suggested that gender role traits could be independent of biology, and further that gender role traits did not have to be either/or, this left the construction of gender more open for interpretation. This, essentially, claimed the territory of gender to be *under construction.*

In the field of psychology, this may be seen as destabilizing gender. The "traditional" theories of Freud and Erikson may be seen to have clear-cut expectations for men: that Ego develop to mediate id and Superego and that the Oedipal stage be worked through. Inherent in these models were ideas and ideals of what it meant to be masculine (independent, strong, individuated, etc.), which gave way to ideas and ideals of what it meant to be feminine (related, passive, dependent, etc.). As these ideas became challenged, in effect, stable notions of what gender

123

and gender role meant were destabilized. With new conceptions of gender and gender role being under construction, there are no longer stable notions, ideas or ideals for being either gender. As Nietzsche or Dostoevski once uttered: "Once God is dead, all things will be possible"[lxxv].

As Chapter Four noted, the field of psychology cannot be considered to be separate from the larger culture in which it finds itself. The point here is that while we may recognize developments in the field of psychology destabilizing gender, we may also recognize these developments as reflections of transitions in the larger culture.

As Chapter Three located the cultural construction of masculinity in social and historical context, it also made note of a crisis in masculinity at each shift. In the mid 19th century as men were changing their workplaces from home-centered guilds and farms to industrial labor and sales labor, the transition from boyhood to manhood became a focal point as noted in the formation of the boy's programs such as the Boy Scouts. Programs like the Boy Scouts intended to "rescue" boys from too much maternal influence and allow boys the chance to be unruly and uncivilized Twainian boys.

In the late 19th/early 20th Century as men's labor became threatened by immigrant labor, trade unions and fraternal organizations sprouted up to protect White Men as well as Christian Men. Kimmel (1993) sites the creation of the KKK and Christian Youth movements as located in the labor struggles of the late 19th/early 20th Centuries.

In the early 20th Century as men were called into service for the Great War, lost their jobs to the Great Depression, and were called into service again for WWII, the absence of the father in the home and the presence of Rosie the Riveter in the factory brought further threats to masculinity. Clinical Psychology was emerging at this time[lxxvi] and this is when the early measures of masculinity and femininity were developed in response to the early 20th Century crisis in masculinity.

The Post-War era found their crisis in masculinity to be rooted in the uprooting of the urban to the decentralized suburbs and shifts in labor from manual to managerial in the 1950s. This redefinition of self in geography, identity, and masculinity is cited by Savran as at the heart of the Beat Generation, a popular culture reconstruction of masculinity.

The late 1960s and early 1970s saw the rise of the Sexual Revolution and the Women's Movement. As women openly challenged the patriarchy and sought to compete with men in the labor market, the structure of the American family was again in transition. Divorce rates were increased as were the absence of fathers. Also at this time was Vietnam, the aftermath of PTSD in returning soldiers, as well as widespread political and countercultural uprisings which forever transformed the landscape of American culture. Masculinity was again in crisis during this era as the nuclear family was redefined and reconstructed. The heirs of this redefinition and resulting shock waves of the Women's Movement, Sexual and student revolutions were the men of the 1980s, who, in the wake of Feminism's question "What does it mean to be a woman in our world today?" posited the question of "what does it mean to be a man in our world today?" These questions were grappled with by not only Robert Bly and his Men's Movement, but also by the various figures depicted by Faludi (1999): the waves of unemployed and underemployed men who ask what their place in the world is now, if not workers; the boys of the Spur Posse who define themselves through sexual activity and openly claim that women have ruined the world; the cadets of the Citadel, whose hazing and aggression may be read as response to the threat of woman; the militias, both political and Christian, who wish to return to the days when men's roles as head of the family and government were unquestioned. These may all be seen as responses to the destabilizing of gender in the wake of Women's Movement, Sexual and other revolutions of the late 1960s and early 1970s.

Each age has had its crisis of masculinity, and each age has reflected that crisis by social programs, psychological measurements, or products of culture. One such product of culture is Metal Glam, which we may recognize as a reflection of the crisis of masculinity of the 1980s as Metal Glam seeks to strengthen masculinity by drawing boundaries of gender tighter in a *boy's only* "club", differentiating traditional gender definitions by lampooning the feminine, and heightening the "traditional" gender roles in espousing the values of hypersexual heterosexualist behavior. In this manner, Metal Glam seeks to re-stabilize gender in response to gender's destabilization.

Fractured Mirror[lxxvii]: Metal Glam as a Reflection of Masculinity in Transition

Following the logic of Gender Theory and the work of Judith Butler (1990), it is proposed here that the influence of cultural and historic changes as framed here culminate in the destabilizing of gender and that Metal Glam is an attempt to reclaim masculinity in its parodying of elements of the feminine while celebrating an exaggerated hypermasculinity. Hence, we may see Metal Glam as a reflection of masculinity in transition from a previous form of "traditional" masculinity (man as worker, doer, maker, breadwinner, economic head of household, emotionally distant) to a masculinity more inclusive and incorporative, as noted by Griswold (1993), Mintz (1998), and Zukerberg (1989). As masculinity is "threatened" and "challenged" by a changing economic environment, shifting roles in the family, shifting members of the family, and changing expectations of gender role, we noted various expressions of the difficulty in transition in the 1980s, such as hypermasculinity in television sitcoms, children's cartoons, GI Joe toys, cinema, and of course, popular music. The destabilization of gender that flows from the cultural changes of the late 1960s and 1970s may be seen in the popular culture as a barometer of culture. Films such as *Mr. Mom* and *Tootsie*, as well as the presence of Boy George, George Michael, and Michael Jackson also may be read as a restructuring of gender presentation and gender role in the 1980s. This restructuring becomes necessary as the previously-held constructs of gender are called into question and dismantled in Kuhnian fashion.

It is proposed here that Metal Glam is not so much along the lines of a Jungian resolution of opposites, but more along the lines of a Piagettian tension between stages of development, or even a Freudian idea of conflict represented in the unconscious that expresses no negative: Metal Glam does not go gently along with the transition in masculinity. The clash in elements and misogyny are not consistent with the idea of resolution or harmonious union, as would be proposed by a Jungian interpretation.

Metal Glam instead may be seen as a reflection of its adolescent audience in the *sturm und drang* of identity and the struggle of development itself. As we note the adolescent audience of the larger genre of Rock and Roll and in turn consider the specific adolescent male audience of Heavy Metal (Walser, 1993; Weinstein, 2000), and as we contemplate the idea of Metal Glam as an attempt to forge a version of masculinity for an audience that is in the process of constructing their own individual identity, including gender identity and gender role identity, we may then see Metal Glam as the struggles of development in the historic era of the 1980s writ large and projected onto the MTV screen and arena stage. Analytic theorists Rosenblum, Daniolos, Kass, and Martin (1999) present in their paper *Adolescents and Popular Culture: A Psychodynamic*

Overview the notion that as Rock and Roll prides itself on its outsider status, it often becomes a vehicle for adolescents who are grappling with issues of development, thus identifying with the outsider status. As popular music is generally current and relevant to its own time[lxxviii], we may read Metal Glam as influenced by and speaking to issues of the shifts in the construction of masculinity. It is hypothesized here that Metal Glam reacts to the challenges to traditional masculinity, at a point in which the adolescent is wrestling with developmental tasks of individual and gender role identity, by trying to maintain a more rigid and traditional construction of masculinity. We may see this is the hypermasculinity and over the top sexuality, as well as misogyny. The stereotyped attributes of the feminine in Metal Glam (the makeup, heels, Spandex) serve to parody the feminine, further strengthening the bonds and homosociality of masculinity, as in the drag show.

Metal Glam may therefore be looked upon as a cultural response to the crisis in masculinity that intersects with an individual's "crisis in masculinity" as developmental tasks of individuation and identity development are grappled with. Metal Glam, then, may serve as an indicator of masculinity in transition for both a culture in the 1980s, as well as a generational cohort, coming of age in the 1980s.

We're An American Band[xxix]: Metal Glam as Specifically American

Not only is the crisis in masculinity particularly American in that the American economy, labor division, social and cultural history are the structural support of the construction of gender in America, but social and historic developments that lead to our hypothesized destabilizing of gender are also particularly American in that the effect of the Sexual Revolution and Women's Movement are largely products of American culture. Aside from this, it is interesting that Metal Glam is a particularly American phenomenon: the overwhelming majority of Metal Glam bands spawned from the Sunset Strip in Los Angeles (Klosterman, 2002b). It is noteworthy that Metal Glam, as the hybrid of two British musical forms, Heavy Metal and British Glam, was firmly rooted in American soil. Part of this, as mentioned above, is that if Metal Glam is a response to the crisis in masculinity, if Metal Glam seeks to restabilize gender, and if the destabilization of gender is perceived in American culture, then it would follow that Metal Glam would be a particularly American phenomenon.

This would be consistent with the theorizing of Hoskyns (1998), who observes that in the 1970s, the American take on British Glam as seen in Kiss and Alice Cooper was more "butch", less gender-bending at its core than David Bowie or T.Rex. In fact, Hoskyns (1998) noted that both Cooper and Kiss moved more into horror and shock tactics, perhaps using violence as an assertion of masculinity.

Although Hoskyns does not take his argument this far, I will propose that American culture was less secure in its masculinity and therefore could be more easily threatened by androgynous and gender-bending presentation. Therefore, American Glam products such as Alice Cooper, Kiss, and the New York Dolls were indeed more "butch" than their British counterparts[lxxx]. Lou Reed was the only American in British Glam camp in the 1970s, and Lou did not wear it well. In the early 1970s, Reed openly declared bisexuality, yet by Sally Can't Dance (Reed, 1974) and Street Hassle (Reed, 1978), Lou had reinvented himself as "butch", homosocial, homophobic, and misogynist[lxxxi].

The argument here is not that American masculine identity was more flappable than British masculine identity, but that the stability of gender role was more fixed in England, and therefore the British culture could stand the gender-bending while America may have been threatened of breaking under the bending. An article by Shaffner (2001), which examines androgynous elements of Indian art, suggests that these androgynous elements are tolerated by Indian culture because the gender roles are clearly defined and stable (Shaffner, 2001). As we have seen in Chapter Three, masculinity, femininity, and gender role have been in constant flux throughout American history. Therefore, with gender roles unstable in and of themselves, Metal Glam appears to be overdetermined: Metal Glam responds to the destabilization of gender in the wake of the Women's Movement and Sexual Revolution by seeking to codify and rigidify masculinity along more "traditional" lines, in order to do so, Metal Glam must differentiate the masculine from the feminine (via make-up and clothing), which is incorporated into the presentation of Metal Glam that serves to lampoon the other and highlight the attributes and values of the masculine in misogyny and hypersexuality. The cultural anxiety that is created in the adoption of androgynous elements, due to the American lack of well-defined gender roles in contrast to British or Indian culture (as suggested by Shaffner, 2001) raises the ante for masculinity, and thus the result is the exaggerated sexuality and misogyny of Metal Glam.

We will now take a closer look at how Metal Glam fits into the theories and cultural observations of authors previously cited in this work.

I'd Rather Be With the Boys[lxxxii]: The Exscription of Women in Metal Glam

It would not be a far stretch to link Rock and Roll with Kimmel's notion of early 20th Century boy culture updated to the late 20th Century. We can see the gang mentality reflected in Mötley Crüe's collective memoir (Strauss, 2002) in which the band members identify themselves as more of a gang than a band. Walser (1993) and Weinstein (2000) also note the exclusion of women from Rock and Roll and Heavy Metal in particular. Walser (1993) particularly frames this as *exscription*, literally, writing women *out* of the genre with the exception of woman as object or woman as threat, or a combination thereof as Walser discusses the role of women as a threatening influence which need be excluded in the Mötley Crüe video "Looks That Kill" (Mötley Crüe, 1986).

The Crüe's Crisis in Masculinity

We may even read the Mötley Crüe saga, as outlined in either their albums (which takes some work and semiotic connecting of the dots within the subcultural context of Heavy Metal) or in their collective memoir, *The Dirt* (Strauss, 2002), as a portrait of masculinity in development: their gang and boyish beginnings, their uncivilized behavior in the House that Crue built above the Rainbow club, their hypersexualized and misogynistic extracurricular (and curricular, this is Rock and Roll we're talking about here) exploits, to their attempts to become fathers themselves. We also see the emasculation of Mick Mars in the 1994 self-titled album's inner fold (see plate 35), where Mick's head placed on the body of centerfold, as well as his castration in the silencing of his guitar-work on Generation Swine. This musical castration was prefigured by the theft of his guitars, as cited in the 1994 liner notes, as well as documented in Strauss (2002: Mars complains vociferously at being silenced as the band moves toward Industrial and away from their trademark Metal Glam guitar sound). We see Nikki's desperate search for his father, and his own struggles with intimacy and fatherhood. We see Vince Neil's misogyny culminate in the death of his daughter and in the only way he could cope with his stress and grief as he acknowledged emotions culturally coded as feminine. We see Tommy in a jail cell, the aftermath of domestic violence, and the aftermath of his homemade pornographic video.

We may also note in the Judas Priest 1981 *Point of Entry* album cover a demasculation via computer paper and five anonymous nameless, faceless blocks. This faceless and nameless appearance contrasts with the songs of rebellion and male bonding within the album, and is quite a departure from the band's usual album covers featuring depictions of power and strength. It is interesting that this emasculating and anonymous album cover should mark Judas Priest's entry into the 1980s, when masculinity is thrown into crisis and gender destabilized.

Fatherhood and the Children of the Beast[lxxxiii]
Griswold (1993) and Blankenhorn's (1995) observations on fatherhood as an aspect of masculinity in American society also may be tied into Metal Glam in relation to the Mötley Crüe collective biography, *The Dirt* (Strauss, 2002). In this collective memoir Mötley Crüe band founder Nikki Sixx draws several connections to the significance of his absent father, his father's absence, as well as his difficulty fathering due to his own absence. Sixx was not alone in his reported difficulties with his father as well as difficulties subsequently fathering as vocal Vince Neil recounts his emotional battle as well as the battle with his own emotions during the death of his daughter, Skylar. Lastly is drummer, Tommy Lee, jailed for domestic violence and removed from his children. These legal difficulties chronologically closely followed the release of a home-made pornographic tape featuring Lee and then-wife Anderson. It would seem that the three principle players in Mötley Crüe each faced a personal crisis in masculinity related to fatherhood, which also tapped into issues of identity, which will see more clearly through the work of David Savran.

Savran's Morrisonification
Savran (1998) links suffering and masochism to an analytic literary position that in suffering and masochism the masculine takes on the position of the feminine. The film *Easy Rider* is analyzed for the martyrdom of Captain America and Billy, including physical beatings, imprisonment, sexuality and gender questioned, and finally death.
Again, the significant aspects of Captain America's and Billy's martyrdom are the vulnerability and softness of the characters, this becomes equated with sexiness (Savran, 1998, pp. 104-105). It will be remembered that culturally at the time of *Easy Rider*'s release (1969) there was a renaissance of popular iconography of Christ as may be seen in Broadway productions *Jesus Christ, Superstar* and *Godspell,* along with best-selling soundtracks in the Rock and Roll market. Hippie pacifist culture also identified with Jesus as a role model. From here is not a far stretch to Jim Morrison who reconstructed the Rock Star as a sacrificial

figure. Morison presented as emotionally vulnerable with songs like "The End" (Doors, 1967/1988), or "When The Music's Over" (Doors, 1969/1988) which featured transparent Oedipal, sexual, violent, and suicidal imagery. Morrison was among the first Rock and Roll performers to writhe in actual or simulated pain during performances, and the self-identification with a messianic figure may be seen in the inner fold of their last album, *L.A. Woman* (Doors, 1971/1988; see plate no 34) in which a modern telephone pole stands in for the crucifix, the imagery of which is punctuated by the mysterious and ominous "Riders on the Storm" which closes the album[lxxxiv], made even more ominous by the announcement of Morrison's death shortly afterwards.

Morrison appears emblematic of not only the reconstructed masculinity as vulnerable, soft, and sexy[lxxxv] but appears influential as a Rock and Roll icon as martyr and sufferer, aspects of which may not only be seen in German-Expressionist influenced art-rockers Ian Curtis of Joy Division and Nick Cave of the Birthday Party (later solo artist), but also in mainstream artists such as Kurt Cobain, Scott Weiland (Stone Temple Pilots), Lane Stamey (Alice in Chains), Trent Reznor (Nine Inch Nails), and Marilyn Manson. This becomes significant in that these latter figures, embodying Griswold'S (1993), Blankenhorn's (1993) and Mintz' (1998) newly constructed sensitive and emotionally present man replaced the Metal Glam Rock Star as the 1980s swept into the 1990s.

Cobain's suicide after Morrisonesque transparent lyrics, the addictions of Weiland and Stamey (as well as Cobain), and the graphic masochism demonstrated in both Marilyn Manson and Nine Inch Nails videos seem wholly different from the preening and posturing of bad boy image of the Metal Glam icon with self-professed misogyny, philandering, and overall sexual indulgence of a shallow nature. It is as though Mötley Crüe and Poison were slapping Burroughs, Keruoac, and Ginsberg with the opera length glove thrown down in challenge for a new masculinity. The Metal Glam ethos does not generally posit the self as victim or the object of suffering or vulnerability, but instead as the one in power, the castrator, the punisher. Yet there is a twist, we do see evidence of vulnerability and suffering in the Power Ballad, the staple of Metal Glam. Here we see sensitivity in Mötley Crüe 's "Home Sweet Home" (Mötley Crüe, 1985), Poison's "Every Rose Has Its Thorn" (Poison, 1988), and Guns N Roses' "November Rain" (Guns N Roses, 1991). We also see an appropriation of the stylistic stereotypic imagery of the feminine in the bright colors, spandex, long-teased hair, make-up and heels. It is as though

Metal Glam's signifiers were symptomatic of the growing pains of a new masculinity under construction, that began with the Beats following WWII and came to fruition in post-Glam Grunge and Industrial. Again the image of Kurt Cobain wearing a dress at MTV's *Headbangers' Ball* gains additional significance.

Cobain's Kaibosh on the Crüe

Klosterman (2002a) notes that the event that signified the end of the Metal Glam era was Grunge band Nirvana's Kurt Cobain appearing on MTV's *Headbanger's Ball* wearing a dress. If Metal Glam fostered a rigid masculinity in its parodying of elements of the feminine, then why would Cobain's drag summon the call to fear the reaper? If gender has been destabilized, which leads to the Metal Glam response of appropriating elements of the feminine to restabilize masculinity, wouldn't Cobain's dress also be a call to arms, opera-length gloves or handbags? Klosterman never deconstructs the imagery of Cobain in a dress on the premier Heavy Metal television format, although based on the conclusions generated above, we may hypothesize that Cobain's overt performance of a destabilized gender may have been read as an acceptance of the cultural imperative to be both sensitive and "manly". Cobain (and Grunge in general) steered clear of themes of hypermasculinity and overt misogyny. Grunge also displayed a version of masculinity that was more consistent with Savran's (1998) thesis of the vulnerable male, the suffering male adopting the masochism and suffering of the feminine as a reconstructed masculinity post World War II. Even the harder edged music of the early 1990s, such as White Zombie, Nine Inch Nails, Marilyn Manson, and Ministry leaned more toward sexual ambiguity, or outright androgyny in the case of Mr. Manson.

It was not that Cobain's drag *caused* an end to the genre of Metal Glam, but that his drag signified a masculinity that was more inclusive and incorporative without the bristly clash in elements that were the trademark of Metal Glam. Cobain's drag signified the end of an era and another plateau of masculinity in transition. Metal Glam, in its format and expressed content of hypersexuality and "traditional" masculinity no longer reflected the cultural consciousness of masculinity. Grunge became the dominant countercultural discourse as its lyric focus was on suffering, vulnerability (Cobain's "Rape Me" (Nirvana, 1993), Soundgarden's "Black Hole Sun" [Soundgarden, 1994]), increased sensitivity, relative lack of misogyny in Grunge ethos, and overall lack of "stardom" and exploitation[lxxxvi].

As The 1980s Fade Away...

It is interesting to note the shift in television as the 1980s move into the 1990s. Long running sitcoms such as *Three's Company* peter out, and the characters of Cheers contemplate marriage and children. A sitcom like *Three's Company,* which relied on sexual innuendo and broad *single entendres* may be seen to be a product of the Sexual Revolution of the late 1960s/early 1970s. *Three's Company*, like the early *Cheers*, traded in misogyny and objectification of women[lxxxvii].

It could be hypothesized that as the 1980s moved into the Blankenhorn like-a-mother-father prescribed traits and attitudes for men, that *Three's Company* could not change its format, and so left the airwaves, while *Cheers* responded to cultural shifts in norms by moving the characters forward: Sam Malone, the principle protagonist of the sitcom, transitions from a womanizing misogynist to a man who begins to wonder out loud how to be masculine in a changing world as he grapples with wanting to father children and marry.

As these changes were enacted on television screens throughout the 1980s into the 1990s, so were they enacted in the realm of Metal Glam from the 1980s into the 1990s. Like Metal Glam, Sam Malone's misogyny is no longer entertaining and must change as the 1980s end and the 1990s begin. Eventually, Metal Glam was unable to tolerate the feminine and masculine blend, and therefore died as gender roles and images shifted in the 1990s. Essentially, Metal Glam became a cultural casualty. More than just a shift in musical style from heavy riffs with a sing-along hook that blend Heavy Metal and British Glam, which fade into minor chords sludigly and sloppily played in alternating dynamics of volume, which became the hallmark of Grunge, the key figures in Metal Glam also suffered their own crises in masculinity, as casualties of their culture, or victims of changes. Dee Snider of Twisted Sister struggled to maintain his role as breadwinner; Mötley Crüe's Nikki Sixx grappled with becoming a father in the face of fatherlessness; also, Vince Neil, also of Mötley Crüe, suffered his own crisis in balancing emotion and nurturance in the face of his daughter, Skylar's death; Judas Priest lead singer and founder Rob Halford struggled with his own public identity and finally came out of the closet and announced his being gay in the Heavy Metal humidity of homophobia (although his band replaced him with someone who sounded just like him, as though they were denying his person and objectifying him). All of these personal experiences that found their way into the music of Heavy Metal and Metal Glam fit nicely into Savran's (1998) thesis of the suffering and increased vulnerability of the new masculinity.

And this brings us back to Kurt Cobain wearing a dress, a symbolic taking on of the feminine outwardly while expressing his inward vulnerability in songs like "Rape Me". Klosterman (2002a) cites this one act as ringing the death knell for Metal Glam. While Cobain most likely did not consciously plan to bring down Metal Glam in one fell off-the-shoulder swoop that night on MTV's *Headbangers' Ball*, one may read this image semiotically as referring to the resolution of the growing pains of the shift in masculinity. Metal Glam's outward appropriation of elements of the feminine in make-up and high heels had been challenged as not masculine enough, as noted in the decline of the "pretty" image in the latter works of Poison, Mötley Crüe , as well as the demise of Quiet Riot and Twisted Sister in the later 1980s, and this image had been replaced with a more muscular and "masculinized" street image suggested by the presentation of Guns N Roses, Skid Row, and Poison and Mötley Crüe 's make-overs (or make-unders as the case may be). Cobain's dress perhaps highlighted the absurdity of the outward appropriation of the aspects of the feminine, perhaps as well as the stylistic clash with the hypermasculinity of Metal Glam. Cobain's presentation of self in drag was consistent in both the outward appropriation of the stylistic elements of the feminine, as well as the inward sensitivity and emotional expression. Cobain represented the new breed or new definition of the masculine, and this was something the Metal Glam players had difficulty reconciling as may be observed by their struggles. This is not say that Cobain or his peers Lane Staley or Scott Weiland were crisis free. In fact they each became their own Morrison, their own brand of suffering artist, but suffering with the growing pains of masculinity may not have been part of their suffering.

Glam Redux: Beyond 1992

Klosterman (2002a) is careful to note that Metal Glam did not suddenly disappear following Kobain's appearance on MTV in 1992, but instead faded away like an overly long guitar solo. True, Grunge did change the face of Rock and Roll from coifed and teased hair to unwashed and somewhat slightly dazed[lxxxviii], but the elements of Glam would resurface in the cyclical nature of popular culture.

Popular culture never really finishes with a trend, it should be remembered, especially in the postmodern consciousness. No, as Punk Rock recombined Rockabilly with S&M, Bondage, Dadaism, the Situationists, and late 1960s/early 1970s radicalism, Metal Glam recombined British Glam with Heavy Metal, borrowing heavily from English cultural forms while appropriating them in a particularly American manner. Just as Metal Glam borrowed from the past, musical movements post-Metal Glam would borrow Metal Glam referents. Nine Inch Nails frontman Trent Reznor became more sleek and stylized following 1994's *Downward Spiral* album (Nine Inch Nails, 1994); the Smashing Pumpkins, Alternative Rock's kingpins in the wake of Nirvana began to present themselves theatrically as more gender-bending, including androgynous stage-wear and eye makeup; Scott Weiland of Stone Temple Pilots performed in Kiss makeup at a show in 1996, and following this was often photographed in eyeliner; and Speedmetal messiahs Metallica mid 1990s efforts Load (Metallica, 1996) and Reload (Metallica, 1997) sport photographs of the band in very glammy attire, including faux fur jackets, eyeliner, and tight shiny pants.

The mid 1990s also marked the advent of a more overtly androgynous style seen in performers like Orgy, Coal Chamber, and of course, Marilyn Manson. And the later 1990s not only saw the reunion of Kiss' original line-up in full makeup (removed in the 1980s when Kiss attempted to compete with the L.A. Metal Glam set, and then later when they attempted to compete with the post-Seattle Heavy Metal scene), and the death and resurrection of Mötley Crüe.

Mötley Crüe in fact, not unlike Kiss, tried to roll with the punches of popular music, trading in their Glam togs for tattoos and shreds in the heyday of Grunge, and then trading in their guitar-riff for loops and samples to fit in with the Industrial movement's Nine Inch Nails, Filter, and Marilyn Manson. By 1999, perhaps fueled by eBay and the nostalgia market, Mötley Crüe had reformed as a Metal Glam act, and in addition to the remastering of the old classics, produced a new album of retroGlam. Not to be outdone by their Metal Glam rivals, Poison released a new album with their original lineup in 2002, as did L.A. Guns.

Perhaps the only band from the Metal Glam era that has been conspicuously absent is Guns N Roses. As Klosterman (2002) and Konow (2003) note, Guns N Roses embodied the Rock and Roll ethic set forth by the New York Dolls: Too Much Too Soon. Guns N Roses fell apart as a band by the time of their fifth release, 1993's *The Spaghetti Incident?*

which, as an album of cover songs, requires the least amount of effort for a band, signifying that the end had come before then. The band's frontman, W. Axl Rose has been working on the next Guns N Roses album *Chinese Democracy* for the last ten years, and although the band will occasionally play (Axl being the only original member left), they have been effectively placed in the "Where Are They Now?" file.

Rock and Roll movements come and go in a cyclical fashion. Elements are recombined and restructured in true postmodern style. At the time of this writing, the current vogue is something of a 1960s Mod revival-inspired proto-Punk movement as seen in the Velvet Underground influences of the Strokes, the Seeds influence in the Hives, and the Television/Patti Smith influence in Sahara Hotnights. In time Metal Glam will work its way back around, repackaged and reformatted for a new generation who have as little idea who Nikki Sixx is as present generations have of who Sid Vicious was.

Rock and Roll All Nite[lxxxix]: Summary and Review

And so we reach the end of our psychological-gender-culture Rock Opera. As in Chapter One, which functioned as an overture, hinting at the themes to be developed and explored later on, this chapter functions as the finale, bringing all the thematic elements to a conclusion. At the outset, our primary focus was on making sense of the clash of elements in Metal Glam of the 1980s, making sense of the hypermasculine, homosocial, and oft-misogynist lyrics and presentation while outfitted in the trappings of stereotyped attributes of the feminine. We looked briefly at the transgression in Rock and Roll in general and note that sex and sexuality have long been text and subtext in the genre of Rock and Roll, youth rebellion, and countercultural movements, from Oscar Wilde to the Surrealists, Elvis Presley, Madonna, Kid Rock[xc], Eminem[xci], and the Donnas[xcii].

We also looked at the intersection between the histories of Heavy Metal, evolving from post-Yardbirds blues-influenced Rock and Roll, merging with Biker and the Altamont incident as the death knell on the Summer of Love. We saw the development of British Glam, also an English-based Rock and Roll movement, having more to do with theatre and fashion than with a winter of discontent. Hoskyns (1998) notes, among other observations, that the London focus of British Glam contrasts with the Northern Industrial focus of Heavy Metal, which has an impact on the formation of Metal Glam in America, originally beginning in the West

Coast's Sunset Strip, yet having great impact in the industrial and rural regions of the country, as noted by Klosterman (2002a), Weinstein (2000), and Walser (1993).

Chapter Two traced the development of Metal Glam as a subgenre of Heavy Metal, yet also deeply influenced by the musical genre of British Glam. A nagging question here was the acceptance of the Metal Glam style by the larger genre of Heavy Metal, which has traditionally been not only heterosexist, but often outright homophobic[xciii] (Walser, 1993; Weinstein, 2000; Konow, 2002). Hoskyns (1998) in tracing the history of 1970s Glam, notes that British Glam has in general been more comfortable with gender-bending and flirting with sexuality than the American bands. An interesting phenomenon takes place in the 1980s, where the New Wave of British Heavy Metal becomes more masculinized in appearance than the American Metal Glam bands that followed them. However, the lyric content and presentation of the American Metal Glam bands contain more misogyny and hypermasculinity than the NWOBHM bands, who focused more on themes of power and the supernatural (Walser, 1993). The upshot of the advent of Metal Glam is thematic a disconnect between the hypermasculine, misogynist presentation of bands such as Mötley Crüe, Poison, Warrant, Britny Fox and Cinderella with their coifed hair, makeovers, and Spandex.

We then examined the social and historical construction of masculinity throughout American history, locating the construction of masculinity as tied into the economy, technology, the urban/suburban landscape, labor, and the structure of the American family. Following was a review of the psychological literature which serves as a reflection of the social and historical lineage of masculinity, as well as responding to crises in masculinity.

I'll Be Damned, Here Comes Your Ghost Again[xciv]: What This All Means to Us in the Here and Now

In grappling with the significance of this theoretical study, it is tempting to conceive of the above work as bound in time and consigned to a small segment of the population: the White, male, adolescent cohort group between ages 13-19 during the years 1983 through 1992. While the focus of this work has been to look at a specific popular culture genre in an historical and cultural context, it will be reminded that history and culture are neither static nor unidirectionally linear: our culture recycles its past and recombines to meet the needs and reflect the tenor of the present times. The 1980s have been enjoying a revival at the time of this writing, boxed sets of compact discs from bands now forgotten and once household words resurface as do television shows, advertisements, and political struggles[xcv]. Nothing ever goes away in our culture: the foot-propelled scooter of the 1950s made a comeback in the late 1990s, the skateboard made a similar comeback as did the Volkswagen Beetle, the Mini, the Vespa, Rockabilly, Swing Music, even street drugs cycle in and out yet never really disappear. *Never Say Die* (Black Sabath, 1979) was the title of Black Sabbath's "last" studio album with frontman Ozzy Osbourne. As recently as 1998 Black Sabbath has released a reunion album (Black Sabbath, 1998) as well as an archival document of live performances (Black Sabbath, 2002). Ozzy himself has enjoyed stardom on his own reality television show. Never say die.

In addition to our culture of recycling, reissuing, and fascination with our own history of popular culture, it should also be reminded that the focus of this work is the concept of masculinity in transition. This is not to suggest that masculinity has arrived at a finished form or absolute state. No, masculinity, indeed the concept of gender itself, may be considered to still be in transition, always evolving, always becoming, but never quite fully being. Savran (1998) and Paglia (1992) quip that gender itself is an elusive and unstable concept, and this should not come as a revelation when conceptualizing of gender and gender role as reflecting and reacting to social, economic, technological, and relational shifts in both culture and the individuals who comprise and are comprised by culture.

Difficult to Cure[xcvi]: Clinical Applications

While Metal Glam's reflection of masculinity in transition may make for interesting reading, the preceding study also has implications and applications for clinical psychology. Perhaps the most immediate application is the consideration of how we in this culture think of what it means to be male or what it means to be female. Regardless of a clinician's theoretic orientation (Orthodox Freudian, strict Behaviorist, Clinical Neuropsychologist, etc.) or relation to the patient or client (assessment, therapy, consultant), the client will always be gendered - perhaps not always in our traditional categories of male or female, but possibly *transgendered* which also incorporates cultural components of gender and being gendered in its transcendence.

Cultural notions of gender and being gendered by culture are so pervasive that even though notions of gender and what it means to be masculine or feminine may not present immediately, these notions are also embedded deeply into the consciousness of the clinician and inform assessment, formulation, and countertransference. In other words, although the patient or client may not present with concerns about what it means to be masculine or feminine, the clinician's regard of the patient or client is subtly and pervasively informed by our cultural notions of gender role, gendered beings, and being gendered.

As every aspect of behavior and presentation is observed by the trained clinician, those observations are shaped and formed by the culture that shapes and informs the clinician. The illustration of the social and cultural history of masculinity in suggests gender has not only been a source of concern throughout American history, but also that gender is not a fixed nor stable construct but subject to change and transformation. Gender becomes "normative" in that we are often not conscious of what *exactly* comprises masculinity or femininity, but may be more like the definition of obscenity, that *we know it when we see it.*

As gender becomes "normative" the cultural constructions of masculinity and femininity become standards of gendered behavior we are unaware of. Unknowingly we refer to these constructs of *masculine* or *feminine* and may use these to compare to a patient or client's behavior, presentation, or concerns. For instance, crying in a man may be thought of as a sign of depression where it may not in a woman; sexually active behavior in a woman may be viewed as pathological or at least a sign of poor judgment while the same may not hold for a man. These admittedly brief examples serve to illustrate the cultural construction of gender-appropriate behavior, a by-product of the cultural construction of gender.

As stated above, gender is not fixed nor stable, and transforms over time due to social, cultural, technological and historical determinants. Although the study focused on Metal Glam of the 1980s, this does not suggest that the 1980s are the only time period where masculinity was in crisis, nor the only time period when gender was under construction. Instead, the Metal Glam of the 1980s was used to illustrate gender in transition in American culture, as a watermark or anthropological artifact. Masculinity in transition could just as easily been demonstrated with the transition in comic books over the past century. The important aspect of this study is the notion of popular culture as a reflection of culture, something of a collective cultural dreamwork in which the aspirations and anxieties of a culture are projected. Just as in the Freudian notion of the dream as a compromise between an unconscious wish and the biological imperative to preserve sleep (Freud, 1999/1900), Metal Glam may be read as a compromise to both ease the tension between masculine and feminine as well as heighten it. The tension spoken of we see illustrated by Falludi (1999), Blankenhorn (1995), Griswold (1993), and Rotundo (1993), Pollack (1998), and Savran (1998) who write of a crisis in masculinity and the notion that masculinity is threatened by the feminine. Metal Glam then serves to incorporate the image of the threatening other, perhaps as a method of gaining power, as well as railing against the feminine in misogyny and exclusion. Metal Glam occurs at a particular place, America, at a particular time, the 1980s, and, like the psychoanalytic formulation of a symptom is overdetermined. The history of masculinity, especially the aspect of masculinity's being in crisis at each and every turn contributes to the gendered presentation of Metal Glam; the shock quality of gender in Metal Glam also contributes, and this may be thought of as the "last frontier" of shock after the gothic-horror approach of Alice Cooper and Kiss. Rock and Roll must maintain its quality of rebellion if it is to survive, its power comes from its outlaw status, and in America in the 1980s, gender and androgyny were ripe for outlaw status in a way they weren't in the 1970s when British Glam swept the UK.

Metal Glam may be seen as the next logical step in the progression of Rock and Roll: from the sexual suggestion of Elvis into the mild androgyny of the Beatles and Mick Jagger, into the drugs and hedonistic free love of the Hippie era to the decadence and indulgence in sex *and* drugs in the first wave of Heavy Metal, the next stop on the shock train could only be the mix of androgyny and misogyny. Needless to say, Metal Glam was not the "final solution" to Rock and Roll and rebellion in America, Speedmetal, Punk, and Hip-Hop would later become shocking and rebellious, and in their own way they were the logical outcome of their determinants. What is significant here is that Metal Glam served as a reflection of American culture, and that this study serves as a model for unpacking and deconstructing popular culture to examine what popular culture can tell us about American culture.

140

Appendix 1: *Coda*[xcvii]

During the research and writing there were be numerous ideas that surfaced, yet were limited by the scope of the study. I would like to be able to briefly acknowledge such ideas, recognizing their significance and the need for further study, while also recognizing that their full exploration would be unwieldy.

Good Old Fashioned Analytic Theory

The symbolic imagery in Metal Glam as relating to archetypal constructs, corresponding to Jung's idea that the androgyne represents an ideal type. Also in this vein was the Freudian idea that Metal Glam symbolically represents a working through of Oedipal conflicts which are reactivated by the *sturm and drang* of adolescence, or even a reawakening of the Kleinian Paranoid-Schizoid position.

Another aspect of Psychoanalytic theory that was tempting to explore under the Savran heading was the notion of Freud as embodying a father figure, with his emphasis on the father in the Oedipal triangle, which parallels to the Christian mythos of a Father-Son-Virgin Mary triangulation. As Christianity has been a dominant force in American culture, the parallels between the mythic organization and Freudian psychology, especially as related to images of the masculine, become seductive areas of study.

Merry Old England and Masculinity

In her corrections and comments, Jill Bloom pointed out that Postwar Industrial England spawned both Heavy Metal as well as British Glam. It would have been interesting to research and speculate the social, cultural, and historic forces that helped shape these two constructions of masculinity in English popular culture, especially as the genres appear to be polar opposites of one another: Heavy Metal with its masculinist ethos and working class identification, and British Glam, which was more urban, dandified, and middle-class in fan and performer base.

The Power Ballad as the Metal Glam Gender Equalizer

In an appendix to Weinstein's Heavy Metal (2000), there is a graph demonstrating the gender differential in Heavy Metal, according to radio requests at California's KROC. Among the interesting findings here was the high numbers of women requesting *lite metal* (Weinstein's term for Metal Glam). This brings up the question of radio and women, as well

141

as the power ballad being a staple of Metal Glam. The first idea being that there may be a gender split in radio listening, with women perhaps listening to the radio more and men perhaps buying albums more. Klosterman (2002) frames this as men being more loyal to bands, which would fit with purchasing albums and keeping them, whereas radio media is very "in the now" and transient, with few attachments to bands.

The second idea this raises is that of the "crossover" song which allows a band to pull in more listeners, going back to Kiss' "Beth". The increased audience share for the "crossover" song is often a female audience, as suggested by both Weinstein (2002) and Walser (1993).

A closer look at the gender split in Metal Glam's audience would be interesting, although this would entail a study in and of itself.

The Function of Androgyny in Rock and Roll

The phenomenon of androgyny in Rock and Roll is long-standing. Rock and Roll evolves from a youth movement to genre in and of itself with its own values and norms, among which is rebellion to dominant culture. Embedded in this is the idea of a cultural id, a cultural unconscious, perhaps even along the lines of Socrates' gadfly. It is significant that no Christian band has ever done well over time (note the demise of Stryper), anything clean or wholesome has been largely a teen marketing gimmick with no lasting power or influence. As Bart Simpson has quipped, "Everyone knows the best bands are affiliated with Satan".

As Rock and Roll positions itself as moving against the grain of the dominant culture, androgyny in Rock and Roll is another facet of Rock and Roll being on the edge in presenting gender on the edge as well. The androgynous, or gender-bending aspects of Rock and Roll go back to Little Richard's flamboyance, Elvis' hips, the Beatles' long hair, Mick Jagger's ambiguous sexuality, to name simply a few the preceded Marc Bolan, David Bowie, Dee Snider, and Nikki Sixx. There was something about the 1980s that brought out a lot of androgyny and sexual ambiguity, including Boy George, George Michael, and Michael Jackson. Granted, these pop icons were tamer forms of gender-bending than Bowie, Mötley Crüe or Poison, but it should be remembered that Pop culture tends to smooth over the contradictions in an effort to sell.

Batman, Rambo, and The Man With No Name

It is interesting to note that the values of the Eriksonian optimally developed person, the individual who was independent, autonomous,

142

industrious, and generative, were also synomous with the values proscribed for the American Male: that he be independent, autonomous, industrious, and generative. These were also the qualities of the Hero, from Tarzan, the Lone Ranger, Superman, Batman, and various other figures of pulp fiction. However, during the 1980s crisis in masculinity, there emerged the what we may consider the dark side of Erikson's developmental model, the stoic silent sufferer, becomes an icon of the 1980s in the cinematic return of Batman, a revival of the Eastwood Man With No Name character, as well as in the creation of Rambo. The shift in the Hero from pre-World War II to post-war may yield some interesting observations about the construction of masculinity as well as the American identity.

What About Rap?

As this study was in its proposal and initial planning stages, Melinda Kulish asked me "What about Rap?". My response was "What *about* Rap?". The implicit question here is how does Rap music and its musical child Hip Hop fit into androgyny, rebellion, and Rock and Roll. I have honestly not given any more thought to this idea than this paragraph, but this is a related idea that would no doubt tap into African American culture and experience as well as the reciprocal relationship between a dominant culture and a non-dominant culture.

Shockabilly Schtick

Perhaps the most gender-bending band in recent years has been the Cramps. Growing out of the 1970s New York City Punk movement, the Cramps embraced the kitsch of the 1950s, including B-Movie horror culture, the exploitation film, hot rods, and sex drugs and Rock and Roll as a threat to the social order. Their chosen/created genre of rockabilly, the most pure form of rock and roll, becomes the subgenre of Punk, Shockabilly. I think the Cramps capture the David Savran shift in the experience of masculinity as illustrated by William S Burroughs and the Beats. It would have been interesting to explore the imagery of the Cramps as a revival, or re-visiting of the Beat era in consideration of the cultural construction of masculinity under construction.

These ideas are truly outside of the scope of this project, but I would like to be able to recognize them formally as they may lead to areas of future study.

References

Ballou, M., & Brown, L.S. (Eds.) (1992) Personality and Psychopathology: Feminist Reappraisals. New York, NY: Guilford Press.

de Beauvoir, S. (1968) The Second Sex. New York, NY: Bantam.

Bem, S.L. (1974). The measurement of psychological androgyny. Journal of Consulting and Clinical Psychology, 42, 155-162.

Bem, S.L., Martyna, W. & Watson, C. (1976). Sex typing and androgyny: Further explorations of the expressive domain. Journal of Personality & Social Psychology Vol 34(5), 1016-1023.

Bem, S.L. (1981) Gender schema theory: A cognitive account of sex typing. Psychological Review, 88(4), 354-364.

Bem, S.L. (1984) Androgyny and gender schema theory: A conceptual and empirical integration. In Nebraska Symposium on Motivation, Vol. 32, (pp. 179-226). Lincoln and London: University of Nebraska Press.

Bem, S.L. (1987a) Yes: Probing the promise of androgyny. In Walsh, M.R. (Ed.) The Psychology of Women: Ongoing Debates, (pp. 206-225). New Haven, CT: Yale University Press.

Bem, S.L. (1987b) No: Gender schema theory and its implications for child development: raising gender-achematic children in a gender-schematic society. In Walsh, M.R. (Ed.) The Psychology of Women: Ongoing Debates (pp. 226-245). New Haven, CT: Yale University Press.

Bergmann, M.S. (1993). Reflections on the history of psychoanalysis. Journal of the American Psychoanalytic Association, 41:929-956.

Bernheimer, C.; & Kahane, (Eds.) (1985). In Dora's Case: Freud, Hysteria, Feminism. New York, NY: Columbia University Press.

Blankenhorn, D. (1995) Fatherless America: Confronting Our Most Urgent Social Problem. New York: Basic.

Blos, P. (1979) The Adolescent Passage: Developmental Issues. New York, NY: International University Press.

Blos, P. (1962). On Adolescence: A Psychoanalytic Interpretation. New York, NY: The Free Press.

Bly, R. (1990). Iron John: A Book About Men. Reading, MA: Addison-Wesley.

Bowie, A.; & Carr, P. (2000). Backstage Passes: Life on the Wild Side With David Bowie. New York: Cooper Square Press.

Butler, J. (1990). Gender Trouble: Feminism and the Subversion of Identity. New York, NY: Routledge, Chapman, & Hall Inc.

Cherlin, A.J. (1998) The Changing American Family and Public Policy. In Cherlin, A.J. (Ed.), The Changing American Family and Public Policy. Washington, D.C.: The Urban Institute Press.

Chodorow, N.J. (1989) Feminism and Psychoanalytic Theory. New Haven, CT: Yale University Press.

Constantinople, A. (1973). Masculinity-femininity: An exception to the famous dictum. Psychological Bulletin,

Derrida, J. (1991). A Derrida Reader (Kamuf, P., Ed.). New York, NY: Columbia University Press.

Deutsch, H. (1944) The Psychology of Women. New York, NY: Grune & Stratton.

Durkheim, E. (1951). Suicide: A Study in Sociology (Spaulding, J.A, & Simpson, G., Trans., Eds.). Glencoe, IL: Free Press.

Erikson, E. (1963). Childhood and Society. New York, NY: Norton.

Erikson, E. (1964). Insight and Responsibility. New York, NY: Norton.

Erikson, E. (1968). Identity: Youth and Crisis. New York, NY: Norton.

Erikson, E. (1979) <u>Identity and the Life Cycle</u>. New York, NY: Norton

Faludi, S. (1999). <u>Stiffed: The Betrayal of the American Man</u>. New York: William & Morrow Company, Inc.

Farganis, S. (1986) <u>The Social Reconstruction of the Feminine Character</u>. Totowa, NJ: Rowman & Littlefield

Foucault, M. (1973). <u>Madness and Civilization: A History of Insanity in the Age of Reason</u> (Howard, r., Trans.). New York, NY: Vintage.

Foucault, M. (1980). <u>The History of Sexuality</u>, Volume 1: An Introduction (R. Hurley, Trans.). New York: Vintage/Random House (Original work in French, 1976).

Frankenberg, R. (1993) <u>White Women, Race Matters: The Social Construction of Whiteness</u>. Minneapolis Press.

Freud, S. (1999) <u>The Interpretation of Dreams</u>. New York, NY: Oxford University Press (J. Crick, Trans.) (Original work published in German in 1900 [1899]).

Freud, S. (1950) <u>Totem and Taboo</u> (J. Strachey, Trans.). New York, NY: Norton. (Original work published in German in 1913).

Freud, S. (1959). <u>Beyond the Pleasure Principle</u> (J. Strachey, Trans.). New York, Bantam. (Original work published in German, 1920).

Freud, S. (1997). The passing of the Oedipal complex. In <u>Sigmund Freud: Sexuality and the Psychology of Love</u> (pp. 166-172). New York: Touchstone, Simon and Schuster, Trans. Riviere. (Original work published in 1924.)

Freud, S. (1997). Some psychological consequences of the anatomical distinction between the sexes. In <u>Sigmund Freud: Sexuality and the Psychology of Love</u> (pp. 173-183). New York: Touchstone, Simon and Schuster, Trans. Strachey. (Original work published in 1925.)

146

Furstenberg, F.F.,Jr. (1998) Good Dads-Bad Dads: Two Faces of Fatherhood. In Cherlin, A.J. (Ed.), The Changing American Family and Public Policy. Waashington, D.C.: The Urban Institute Press.

Gay, P. (1988). Freud: A Life For Our Time. New York, NY: Norton.

Gilligan, C. (1982) In a Different Voice: Psychological Theory and Women's Development. Cambridge, MA: Harvard University Press.

Ginsburg, H.P., & Opper, S. (1988). Piaget's Thoery of Intellectual Development (Third Ed.). New Jersey: Prentice Hall.

Green, B.L. & Kenrick, D.T. (1994). The attractiveness of gender-typed traits at different relationship levels: Androgynous characteristics may be desirable after all. Personality and Social Psychology Bulletin, 20(3), 244-253.

Griswold, R.L. (1993) Fatherhood in America: A History. New York: Basic.

Handelman, D., Pond, S. (1987) Money for nothing and the chicks for free: On the road with Mötley Crüe. Rolling Stone, Aug 13, 1987.

Hebdige, D. (1979). Subculture: The Meaning of Style. London and New York: Routledge.

Hathaway, S.R.; & McKinley, J.C. (1989) Minnesota Multiphasic Personality Inventory – 2. Minneapolis, MN: University of Minnesota Press.

Hopkins, J., & Sugerman, D. (1995) No One Here Gets Out Alive. (Rev. ed.) New York: Warner.

Horney, K. (1967) Feminine Psychology. New York, NY: Norton.

Hoskyns, B. (1998). Glam! Bowie, Bolan and the Glitter Rock Revolution. London: Faber & Faber Ltd.

147

Jung, C.G. (1977). Anima and Animus. In Two Essays on Analytical Psychology. In Head, H., Fordham, M., Adler, G., and McGuire, W. (Eds.) The Collected Works of C.G. Jung, Vol 7, Bollingen Series XX (pp. 188-211), Princeton University Press, New Jersey. Trans. R.F.C. Hull. (Original work published in 1934).

Jung, C.G. (1980). Aion: Researches into the Phenomenology of the Self. In Head, H., Fordham, M., Adler, G., and McGuire, W. (Eds.) The Collected Works of C.G. Jung, Vol 9, Part 2, Bollingen Series XX, Princeton University Press, New Jersey. Trans. R.F.C. Hull. (Original work published in 1959).

Jung, C.G. (1980). Psychology and Alchemy. In Head, H., Fordham, M., Adler, G., and McGuire, W. (Eds.) The Collected Works of C.G. Jung, Vol 12, Bollingen Series XX, Princeton University Press, New Jersey. Trans. R.F.C. Hull. (Original work published in 1953).

Jung, C.G. (1983). Psychiatric Studies. In Head, H., Fordham, M., Adler, G., and McGuire, W. (Eds.) The Collected Works of C.G. Jung, Vol 1, Bollingen Series XX, Princeton University Press, New Jersey. Trans. R.F.C. Hull. (Original work published in 1957).

Jung, C.G. (1989). Mysterium Coniunctionis. In Head, H., Fordham, M., Adler, G., and McGuire, W. (Eds.) The Collected Works of C.G. Jung, Vol 14, Bollingen Series XX, Princeton University Press, New Jersey. Trans. R.F.C. Hull. (Original work published in 1963).

Jung, C.G. (1990). The Archetypes and the Collective Unconscious. In Head, H., Fordham, M., Adler, G., and McGuire, W. (Eds.) The Collected Works of C.G. Jung, Vol 9, Part 1, Bollingen Series XX, Princeton University Press, New Jersey. Trans. R.F.C. Hull. (Original work published in 1959).

Kasson, J.F. (1990). Rudeness and Civility: Manners in Nineteenth Century Urban America. New York, NY: Hill and Wang.

Katz, J.N. (1995) The Invention of Heterosexuality. New York, NY: Dutton.

Kegan, R. (1982) The Evolving Self. Cambridge, MA: Harvard University Press.

Kimmel, M. (1996). Manhood in America: A Cultural History. New York: Free Press.

Kinney, DA. (1999). From "headbangers" to "hippies": Delineating adolescents' active attemts to form an alternative peer culture. In McLellan, J.A., (Ed.), The Role of Peer Groups in Adolescent Social Identity: Exploring the Importance of Stability and Change (pp. 21-35). San Francisco, CA: Jossey-Bass.

Kitts, J. (1994). Kisstory. New York: Kisstory, LTD.

Klein, M. (1948). Contributions to Psychanalysis: 1921-1945. London: Hogarth Press.

Klosterman, C. (2002a) Fargo Rock City: A Heavy Metal Odyssey in Rural North Dakota. NY: Touchstone.

Klosterman, C. (2002b) Paradise city. Spin, September 2002.

Kohlberg, L.A. (1966). "A cognitive developmental analysis of children's sex roles, concepts, and attitudes." In E.E. Maccoby (Ed.) The Development of Sex Differences. Stanford, CA: Standford University Press.

Kohlberg, L.A. (1969) Stage and sequence: The cognitive developmental approach to socialization. In Goslin (Ed.,) Handbook of Socialization: Theory and Research. New Yoirk, Rand McNally.

Kohlberg, L.A. (1984). The Psychology of Moral Development, Vol II of Essays on Moral Development. San Francisco, CA: Harper and Row.

Kohlberg, L.A; & Zeigler, E. (1967). The impact of cognitive maturity on the development of sex role attitudes in the years of four to eight. Genetic Psychology Mongraphs, 1965, 75, 89-165.

Konow, D. (2002). Bang Your Head: The Rise and Fall of Heavy Metal. New York, NY: Three Rivers Press.

Lacan, J. (1982). Feminine Sexuality. (J. Rose, Trans.) New York: Norton.

Lasky, R. (1993). Dynamics of Development and the Therapeutic Process. Northvale, New Jersey: Jason Aronson, Inc.

Leahy, R. L., and Eiter, M. (1980) Moral judgment and the development of real and ideal androgynous self-image during adolescence and adulthood. Developmental Psychology 16(4), 362-370.

Lendt, C.K. (1997) Kiss And Sell: The Making of a Supergroup. New York, NY: Billboard Books.

Lorenzi-Cioldi, F. (1996). Psychological androgyny: A concept in search of lesser substance. Towards the understanding of the transformation of a social representation. Journal for the Theory of Social Behaviour, 26(2), 137-155.

Lowry, R. S. (1997), Domestic interiors: Boyhood nostalgia and affective labor in the gilded age. In Pfister, J.; Sharg, N, Eds.) Inventing the Psychological. New Haven, CT: Yale University Press.

McNeil, L.; & McCain, G. (Eds.) (1997). Please Kill Me: The Uncensored Oral History of Punk. New York, NY: Penguin.

Manson, M. (1999) Columbine: Whose fault is it? Rolling Stone, 815, June 24, 1999.

Marcus, G. (1989) Lipstick Traces: A Secret History of the Twentieth Century. Cambridge, MA: Harvard University Press.

Marsh, H.W. (1987). Masculinity, femininity and androgyny : Their relations with multiple dimensions of self-concept. Multivariate Behavioral Research, 22, 91-118.

Marsh, H.W., & Byrne, B.M. (1991). Differentiated additive androgyny model: Relations between masculinity, famininity, and multiple dimensions of self-concept. Journal of Personality and Social Psychology. Vol. 61, No. 5, 811-828.

Mintz, S. (1998). From patriarchy to androgyny and other myths: Placing men's family roles in historical perspective. In Booth, A., and Crouter, A.C. (Eds.) Men in Families: When Do They Get Involved? What Difference Does it Make? (pp. 3-30). New Jersey: Lawrence Erlbaum Associates.

Morrison, G. (1989) Arkham Asylum: A Serious House on Serious Earth. New York, NY: DC Comics, Warner Communications.

Neely, K. (1992). Axl Rose. Rolling Stone, 641, Oct. 15, 1992.

Obrecht, J. (1980). Eddie Van Halen: Young wizard of power rock. Guitar Player, April, 1980.

Paglia, C. (1992). Sex, Art, and American Culture. New York, NY: Vintage.

Pfister, J. &S harg, N. (Eds.) (1997). Inventing the Psychological. New Haven, CT : Yale University Press.

Piaget, J. (1926) The Language and Thought of the Child (M. Gabain, Trans.) London : Routledge and Keagan Paul.

Piaget, J. (1954). The Construction of Reality in the Child (M. Cook, Trans). New York: Basic.

Piaget, J. (1958). The Growth of Logical Thinking from Childhood to Adolescence (A. Parsons, S. Seagrin, Trans.) New York : Basic

Pollack, W. (1998). Real Boys: Rescuing Our Sons From the Myths of Boyhood. New York: Owl/Henry Holt.

Powell, G.N. & Butterfield, D.A. (1989). The "good manager": Did androgyny fare better in the 1980s? Groups and Organization Studies, Vol. 14, No. 2, June 1989, 216-233. Sage Publications.

Real, T. (1997) I Don't Want to Talk About It: The Secret of Male Depression. New York, NY: Fireside/Simon & Schuster.

Rosenblum, D.S.; Daniolos, P.; Kass, N.; & Martin, A. (1999). Adolescents and popular culture: A psychodynamic overview. The Psychoanalytic Study of the Child, Vol. 54, 319-338.

Rotundo, E.A. (1993). American Manhood: Transformations In Masculinity From the Revolution To the Modern Era. New York: Basic.

Savran, D. (1998) Taking it Like a Man: White Masculinity, Masochism, and Contemporary American Culture. New Jersey: Princeton University Press.

Schaffner, B. (2001) Androgyny in Indian art and culture: Psychoanalytic implications. Journal of the American Academy of Psychoanalysis, 29(1), 113-125.

Shaver, P.R., Papalia, D., Clark, C.L., Koski,, L.R., Tidwell, M.C., & Nalbone, D. (1996). Androgyny and attachment security: Two related models of optimal personality. Personality and Social Psychology Bulletin, 22(6), 582-597.

Singer, J. (1997). Androgyny: The Opposites Within. York Beach, ME: Nicholas-Hays. (Originally published in 1976).

Stake, J.E., Zand, D. & Smalley, R. (1996). The relation of instrumentality and expressiveness to self-concept and adjustment: A social context perspective. Journal of Social and Clinical Psychology, 15(2), 167-190.

Strauss, N. (Ed.) (2002). The Dirt: Mötley Crüe. NY: Regan/Harper Collins.

Spence, J.T. (1984). Gender identity and its implications for the concepts of masculinity and feminity. In Nebraska Symposium on Motivation, Vol. 32, (pp. 61-95). Lincoln and London: University of Nebraska Press.

Sulloway, F.J. (1992). Freud, Biologist of the Mind: Beyond the Psychoanalytic Legend. Cambridge, MA: Harvard University Press.

Thompson, H.S. (1967). Hell's Angels: A Strange and Terrible Saga. New York: Random House.

Walser, R. (1993). Running With the Devil: Power, Gender, and Madness in Heavy Metal Music. Hanover, NH: University Press of New England/Wesleyan University Press.

Weber, M. (2002) The Protestant Ethic and the Spirit of Capitalism (Kalberg, S., Trans., Ed.). Los Angeles, CA: Roxbury Publishing Company.

Weinstein, D. (2000) Heavy Metal: The Music and its Culture. Da Capo Press.

Wilcove, J.L. (1998). Perceptions of masculinity, femininity, and androgyny among a select cohort of gifted adolescent males. Journal for the Education of the Gifted, 21(3), 288-309.

Zukerberg, R.M. (1989). From John Wayne to Tootsie: The Masculine Struggle with Psychological Integration, in Gender in Transition, Offerman-Zuckerberg, J., Ed. New York, NY: Plenum.

Recordings Referenced:
AC/DC (1979) Highway To Hell [compact disc]. New York, NY: Atlantic Records/Atco.

AC/DC (1980) Back In Black [compact disc]. New York, NY: Atlantic Records/Atco.

Be-Bop DeLuxe (1974). Axe Victim [compact disc]. New York, NY: Harvest/EMI International. (Originally recorded in 1974, remastered and re-released in 1990.)

Black Sabbath (1970a). Black Sabbath [compact disc]. New York, NY: Warner Bros. Records.

Black Sabbath (1970b). Paranoid [compact disc]. New York, NY: Warner Bros. Records.

Black Sabbath (1971) Master of Reality [compact disc]. New York, NY: Warner Bros. Records.

Black Sabbath (1972) Vol. 4 [compact disc]. New York, NY: Warner Bros. Records.

Black Sabbath (1974). Sabbath, Bloody Sabbath [compact disc]. New York, NY: Warner Bros. Records.

Black Sabbath (1975). Sabotage [compact disc]. New York, NY: Warner Bros. Records.
Black Sabbath (1976). Technical Ecstasy [compact disc]. New York, NY: Warner Bros. Records.

Black Sabbath (1978). Never Say Die! [compact disc]. New York, NY: Warner Bros. Records.

Black Sabbath (1994). Nativity in Black: A Tribute to Black Sabbath [performed by various artists). [compact disc]. New York, NY: Columbia Records.

Black Sabbath (1998). Reunion [compact disc]. New York, NY: Sony Entertainment.

Black Sabbath (2000). Nativity in Black II: A Tribute to Black Sabbath [performed by various artists]. [compact disc]. Hollywood, CA: Divine Records.

Black Sabbath (2002). Past Lives [compact disc]. New York, NY: Divine Recordings/Sanctuary.

Bowie, David (1969) Space Oddity [compact disc]. Salem, MA: Rykodisc. (Originally recorded in 1969 under RCA/Mainman, remastered and re-released in 1990.)

Bowie, David (1970) <u>The Man Who Sold The World</u> [compact disc]. Salem, MA: Rykodisc. (Originally recorded in 1970 and released in 1972 under RCA/Mainman, remastered and re-released in 1990.)

Bowie, David (1971). <u>Hunky Dory</u> [compact disc]. Salem, MA: Rykodisc. (Originally recorded in 1971 under RCA/Mainman, remastered and re-released in 1990.)

Bowie, David (1972). <u>The Rise and Fall of Ziggy Stardust and the Spiders From Mars: 30th Anniversary Edition</u> [compact disc]. Jones/Tintoretto Entertainment Co., Ltd. (Originally recorded in 1972 under RCA Mainman, remastered and released in 2002.)

Bowie, David (1973). <u>Alladin Sane</u> [compact disc]. Salem, MA: Rykodisc. (Originally recorded in 1973 under RCA/Mainman, remastered and re-released in 1990.)

Bowie, David (1973). <u>Pinups</u> [compact disc]. Salem, MA: Rykodisc. (Originally recorded in 1973 under RCA/Mainman, remastered and re-released in 1990.)

Bowie, David (1974). <u>Diamond Dogs</u> [compact disc]. Salem, MA: Rykodisc. (Originally recorded in 1974 under RCA/Mainman, remastered and re-released in 1990.)

Britny Fox (2001). <u>The Best of Britny Fox</u> [compact disc]. New York, NY: Metal Masters Series, Legacy/Sony Music Entertainment.

Cinderella (1988). <u>Long Cold Winter</u> [compact disc]. New York, NY: Mercury/Polygram Records.

Deep Purple (1972). <u>Machine Head</u> [compact disc]. New York, NY: Warner Bros. Records.

Doors, The (1988). <u>The Doors</u> [compact disc]. New York, NY: Elektra Records. (Original work recorded 1967, released on compact disc 1988.)

Doors, The (1969) <u>Waiting for the Sun</u> [compact disc]. New York, NY: Elektra Records. (Original work recorded 1969, released on compact disc 1988.)

Doors, The (1971) <u>L.A. Woman</u> [compact disc]. New York, NY: Elektra Records. (Original work recorded 1971, released on compact disc 1988.)

Faster Pussycat (1987). <u>Faster Pussycat</u> [compact disc]. New York, NY: Elektra/Asylum Records/Warner Communications.

Faster Pussycat (1992). <u>Whipped!</u> [compact disc]. New York, NY: Elektra Entertainment/Warner Communications.

Guns N Roses (1987). <u>Appetite for Destruction</u> [compact disc]. New York, NY: Uzi Suicide/Geffen Records/Warner Communications.

Guns N Roses (1991). <u>Use Your Illusion I</u> [compact disc]. New York, NY: Uzi Suicide/Geffen Records/Warner Communications.

Guns N Roses (1993) "<u>The Spaghetti Incident?</u>" [compact disc]. New York, NY: Uzi Suicide/Geffen Records/Warner Communications.

Iron Butterfly (1968). <u>In-A-Gadda-Da-Vida</u> [compact disc]. New York, NY: Rhino/Atlantic & Atco Remasters. (Originally released in 1968 on Atco (Atlantic Recordings), remastered in 1995, Rhino/Atlantic.)

Iron Maiden (1980). <u>Killers</u> [compact disc]. Iron Maiden Holdings, Ltd. (Originally released in 1980 under EMI, remastered and re-released in 1998.)

Iron Maiden (1981). <u>The Number of the Beast</u> [compact disc]. Iron Maiden Holdings, Ltd. (Originally released in 1981 under EMI, remastered and re-released in 1998.)

Judas Priest (1977) <u>Sin After Sin</u> [compact disc]. New York, NY: Columbia/Legacy/Sony. (Originally recorded in 1977, remastered in 2001.)

Judas Priest (1978) Stained Class [compact disc]. New York, NY: Columbia/Legacy/Sony. (Originally recorded in 1978, remastered in 2001.)

Judas Priest (1979a). Hell Bent for Leather [compact disc]. New York, NY: Columbia/Legacy/Sony. (Originally recorded in 1979, remastered in 2001.)

Judas Priest (1979b). Unleashed In The East [compact disc]. New York, NY: Columbia/Legacy/Sony. (Originally recorded in 1979, remastered in 2001.)

Judas Priest (1980). British Steel [compact disc]. New York, NY: Columbia/Legacy/Sony. (Originally recorded in 1980, remastered in 2001.)

Judas Priest (1981). Point of Entry [compact disc]. New York, NY: Columbia/Legacy/Sony. (Originally recorded in 1981, remastered in 2001.)

Kiss (1974a). Kiss [compact disc]. New York, NY: Casablanca/Polygram.

Kiss (1974b). Hotter Than Hell [compact disc]. New York, NY: Casablanca/Polygram.

Kiss (1975a). Dressed to Kill [compact disc]. New York, NY: Casablanca/Polygram.

Kiss (1975b). Alive! [compact disc]. New York, NY: Mercury Records/Kiss Catalog, Ltd.

Kiss (1976a). Destroyer [compact disc]. New York, NY: Casablanca/Polygram.

Kiss (1976b). Rock and Roll OVer [compact disc]. New York, NY: Casablanca/Polygram.

Kiss (1977a). Love Gun [compact disc]. New York, NY: Casablanca/Polygram.

Kiss (1977b). <u>Alive II</u> [compact disc]. New York, NY: Mercury Records/Kiss Catalog, Ltd.

Kiss (1979). <u>Dynasty</u> [compact disc]. New York, NY: Casablanca/Polygram.

Kiss (1981). <u>(Music From) The Elder</u> [compact disc]. New York, NY: Casablanca/Polygram.

Kiss (1982). <u>Creatures of the Night</u> [compact disc]. New York, NY: Casablanca/Polygram.

Kiss (1983). <u>Lick It Up</u> [compact disc]. New York, NY: Mercury Records/Kiss Catalog, Ltd.

Kiss (1985). <u>Asylum</u> [compact disc]. New York, NY: Mercury/Polygram.

Kiss (1987). <u>Crazy Nights</u> [compact disc]. New York, NY: Mercury Records/Kiss Catalog, Ltd.

L.A. Guns (1988). <u>L.A. Guns</u> [compact disc]. New York, NY: Vertigo Records/Polygram Records.

L.A. Guns (1989). <u>Cocked & Loaded</u> [compact disc]. New York, NY: Vertigo Records/Polygram Records.

L.A. Guns (1991). <u>Hollywood Vampires</u> [compact disc]. New York, NY: Polydor/Polygram Records, Inc.

L.A. Guns (2001) <u>Man in the Moon</u> [compact disc]. Los Angeles: CA. Eagle Rock Entertainment/Spitfire Records.

Led Zeppelin (1971) <u>Led Zeppelin IV (Runes)</u> [compact disc]. New York, NY: Atlantic Recording Corporation (Original work released 1971, re-released 1991).

Metallica (1983) <u>Kill'Em All</u> [compact disc]. New York, NY: Elektra/Time Warner.

Metallica (1986) <u>Master of Puppets</u> [compact disc]. New York, NY: Elektra/Time Warner.

Metallica (1988) <u>...And Justice For All</u> [compact disc]. New York, NY: Elektra/Time Warner.

Metallica (1991) <u>Metallica</u> [compact disc]. New York, NY: Elektra Entertainment/Warner Communications.

Metallica (1996) <u>Load</u> [compact disc]. New York, NY: Elektra Entertainment/Warner Communications.

Metallica (1997) <u>Metallica</u> [compact disc]. New York, NY: Elektra Entertainment/Warner Communications.

Ministry (1989) <u>The Mind is a Terrible Thing to Taste</u> [compact disc]. New York, NY: Sire/Warner Bros. Inc.

Misfits (1980) <u>Earth A.D.</u> [compact disc]. New York, NY: Caroline.

Misfits (1997) <u>Static Age</u> [compact disc]. New York, NY: Caroline. (Originally recorded in 1978, re-released in 1997).

Monster Magnet (2001) <u>God Says No</u> [compact disc]. New York, NY: A&M Records.

Mötley Crüe (1981). <u>Too Fast For Love</u> [compact disc]. New York NY: Mötley Records/Beyond Music. (Original work released 1981, remastered 1999.)

Mötley Crüe (1983). <u>Shout at the Devil</u> [compact disc]. New York NY: Mötley Records/Beyond Music. (Original work released 1983, remastered 1999.)

Mötley Crüe (1985). <u>Theatre of Pain</u> [compact disc]. New York, NY: Elektra/Asylum Records.

Mötley Crüe (1987). <u>Girls, Girls, Girls</u> [compact disc]. New York, NY: Mötley Records/Beyond Music. (Original work released 1987, remastered 1999.)

Mötley Crüe (1989). <u>Dr. Feelgood</u> [compact disc]. New York, NY: Mötley Records/Beyond Music. (Original work released 1989, remastered 1999.)

Mötley Crüe (1994) <u>Mötley Crüe</u> [compact disc]. New York, NY: Elektra Entertainment/Mötley Records.

Mötley Crüe (1997). <u>Generation Swine</u> [compact disc]. New York, NY: Elektra Entertainment/Mötley Records.

Mötley Crüe (2000). <u>New Tattoo</u> [compact disc]. New York, NY: Mötley Records/Beyond Music.

Nine Inch Nails (1994) <u>The Downward Spiral</u> [compact disc]. New York, NY: Interscope/Nothing Inc.

Nirvana (1991). <u>Nervermind</u> [compact disc]. Los Angeles, CA: The David Geffen Company/SubPop.

Nirvana (1993). <u>In Utero</u> [compact disc]. Los Angeles, CA: The David Geffen Company/SubPop.

Pink Floyd (1975). <u>Wish You Were Here</u> [compact disc]. New York, NY: EMI Recordings (Original work released 1975, re-mastered 1992, re-released 1994).

Pink Floyd (1979). <u>The Wall</u> [compact disc]. New York, NY: EMI Recordings (Original work released 1979, re-mastered 1992, re-released 1994).

Poison (1986). <u>Look What The Cat Dragged In</u> [compact disc]. Hollywood CA: Capitol Records.

Poison (1988). <u>Open Up and Say…Ahh!</u> [compact disc]. Hollywood CA: Enigma Records/Capitol Records.

Poison (1990). Flesh & Blood [compact disc]. Hollywood CA: Enigma Records/Capitol Records.

Posion (1993). Native Tongue [compact disc]. Hollywood, CA: Capitol Records, Inc.

Poison (2000). Crack a Smile...And More! [compact disc]. Hollywood, CA: Capitold Records, Inc.

Poison (2002). Hollyweird [compact disc]. Los Angeles, CA: Cyanide Records.

Police (1983). Synchronicity [record]. New York, NY: A&M Records.

Quiet Riot (1983) Metal Health [compact disc]. New York: Portrait/Epic/Sony. (Originally released in 1983, remastered and re-released as part of Sony's *Metal Masters Series* in 2001).

Reed, Lou. (1972). Transformer. New York, NY: RCA Records. (Originally released 1972, remastered and released 1998, BMG Entertainment International, Ltd.

Reed, Lou (1974). Sally Can't Dance [compact disc]. New York, NY: RCA/BMG. (Originally released in 1974 under RCA/Mainman, remastered and re-released in 2001.)

Reed, Lou (1978). Street Hassle [compact disc]. New York, NY: Arista Records.

Rolling Stones (1973) Goats Head Soup [compact disc]. Beverly Hills, CA: Rolling Stones Records/Virgin Records America.

Skid Row (1989) Skid Row [compact disc]. New York, NY: Atlantic Recording Corporation.

Slade (1993). Sladest [compact disc]. London, England: Polydor UK. (Original material recorded in 1970, 1971, 1972, and 1973.)

Soundgarden (1994) <u>Superunknown</u> [compact disc]. New York, NY: A&M Records.

Suicidal Tendencies (1983) <u>Suicidal Tendencies</u> [compact disc]. Sun Valley, CA: Frontier Records. (Originally released in 1983, re-released in 1997 on Epitaph.)

Suicidal Tendencies (1987) <u>Join The Army</u> [compact disc]. Los Angeles, CA: Plan 9/Caroline Records.

Sweet (2000) <u>The Sweet: Greatest Hits</u> [compact disc]. BMG Entertainment International/UK & Ireland. (Original material recorded in 1971, 1972, 1973, 1974, and 1975.)

Thunders, Johnny (1988) <u>Hurt Me</u> [compact disc]. Paris, France: New Rose Records.

T. Rex (1971). <u>Electric Warrior</u> [compact disc]. New York, NY: Reprise Records/Warner Bros.

T. Rex (1972). <u>The Slider</u> [compact disc]. Relativity. (Originally released 1972, re-released 1987 licensed by Marc On Wax, Ltd.

Warrant (1989). <u>Dirty Rotten Filthy Stinking Rich</u> [compact disc]. New York, NY: Columbia Records/Sony Music Entertainment.

<u>Video Media Referenced:</u>
Deane, Elizabeth (Executive Producer). (1995) <u>Rock & Roll</u> [video, 10 episode documentary]. (Available through PBS/WGBH Boston)

Debonne, Y.; & Santiago, C. (Directors). (2000) <u>VH1 Behind the Music: Mötley Crüe.</u> [Television documentary available on DVD] (Available through BMG Video).

Gaspin, J., Zalaznick, L., & Ginsburg, M. (Executive Producers). (2000) <u>Rock Story: Censorship</u> [video series, documentary]. (Available through VH1 Productions). (Original air date: March 29, 2000, 10:00 pm ET/PT).

Guest, C.; McKean, M.; Reiner, R.; & Shearer, H. (1984) This Is Spinal Tap [Digital video disc]. Metro Goldwyn Mayer/Embassy Home Entertainment.

Moll, G. (Executive Producer) (1999) Behind the Music: Ozzy Osbourne [video documentary]. (Available from VH1 Home Entertainment.)

Mötley Crüe (Featured artist). (1986) Mötley Crüe: Uncensored [Video compilation]. (Available from Elektra Entertertainment, Elektra/Asylum Records/Warner Communications)

Pennbaker, D.A. (Director) (1984). Ziggy Stardust and the Spiders From Mars. [Video] RCA Video Productions/Columbia Pictures Home Video.

Spheeris, P. (Director); Dayton, J., & Faris, V. (Producers). (1988). The Decline of Western Civilization Part II: The Metal Years [Film]. New Line Cinema. (Available from RCA/Columbia Pictures Home Video). (Original film release 1988, video released 1989.)

Warrant (Featured artist). (1991) Warrant: Cherry Pie, Quality You Can Taste [video compilation]. (Available from Sony Music Entertainment)

Lyric References:
Adler, S., McKagan, D., Rose, A., Slash, & Stradlin, I. (1987) It's so easy [recorded by Guns N Roses]. On: Appetite for Destruction [compact disc]. New York NY: Uzi Suicide/Geffen/Warner Communications.

Bonfire, M. (1968) Born to be wild [recorded by Steppenwolf]. On: Steppenwolf [vinyl] New York, NY: Stateside.

Bowie, D. (1969) Space odditiy [recorded by David Bowie]. On: Space Oddity [compact disc] Virgin/EMI. (Originally released in 1969, re-released in 1990 under Rykodisc, remastered and re-released as Virgin/EMI in 1999.)

Bowie, D. (1972) All the young dudes [recorded by Mott the Hoople]. On: All The Young Dudes [compact disc] New York, NY: Atlantic

Records/Columbia Records/Legacy/Sony Music. (Originally released in 1972, re-released in 1992.)

Dall, B., DeVille, C.C., Michaels, B., & Rockett, R. (1986). Talk dirty to me [recorded by Poison]. On: <u>Look What the Cat Dragged In</u> [compact disc]. Hollywood CA: Capitol Records.

Dall, B., DeVille, C.C., Michaels, B., & Rockett, R. (1988). Nothin' but a good time [recorded by Poison]. On: <u>Open Up and Say…Ahh!</u> [compact disc]. Hollywood CA: Enigma Records/Capitol Records.

Downe, T. (1987a) Bathroom wall [recorded by Faster Pussycat]. On: <u>Faster Pussycat</u> [compact disc]. New York NY: Electra/Asylum Records/Warner Communications.

Downe, T. (1987b) Cathouse [recorded by Faster Pussycat]. On: <u>Faster Pussycat</u> [compact disc]. New York NY: Electra/Asylum Records/Warner Communications.

Holder, N.& Lea, J. (1973) Cum on feel the noize [recorded by Slade]. On: <u>Sladest</u>. New York: Polydor Records (Originally released as a single in 1973, re-released as part of a compilation album in 1993).

Jagger, M. & Richard, K. (1964) Satisfaction [recorded by the Rolling Stones]. On <u>The London Years</u> [compact disc]. EMI International Recordings (Originally released as a single in 1964 on London Records).

Jagger, M. & Richard, K. (1967). Let's spend the night together [recorded by the Rolling Stones]. On <u>The London Years</u> [compact disc]. EMI International Recordings (Originally released as a single in 1967 on London Records).

Jagger, M. & Richard, K. (1973). Star star [recorded by the Rolling Stones]. On <u>Goat's Head Soup</u> [compact disc]. Beverly Hills, CA: Rolling Stones Records/Virgin Records America.

Neilsen, R. (1978) Surrender [recorded by Cheap Trick]. On: Heaven Tonight [compact disc]. New York, NY: Epic Records/CBS Inc. (Originally released 1978, released 1992).

Page, J. & Plant, R. (1971) <u>Stairway to Heaven</u> [recorded by Led Zeppelin]. On: <u>Led Zeppelin IV (Runes)</u>. Atlantic Recording Corporation.

Reed, L. (1972) Make up [recorded by Lou Reed] on *Transformer*. New York, NY: RCA Records. (Originally released 1972, remastered and released 1998, BMG Entertainment International, Ltd.

Reed, L. (1978). Street hassle [recorded by Lou Reed]. On: <u>Street Hassle</u> [compact disc]. New York, NY: Arista Records.

Sixx, N., & Neil, V. (1982). Ten seconds to love [recorded by Mötley Crüe]. On: <u>Shout at the Devil</u> [compact disc]. Los Angeles CA: Mötley Records/Beyond Music/BMG. (Originally released 1983, remastered 1999.)

Sixx, N. (1989) Kickstart my heart [recorded by Mötley Crüe]. On: <u>Dr. Feelgood</u> [compact disc]. Los Angeles CA: Mötley Records/Beyond Music/BMG. (Originally released 1989, remastered 1999.)

Sixx, N. & Mars, M. (1989) Slice of your pie [recorded by Mötley Crüe]. On: <u>Dr. Feelgood</u> [compact disc]. Los Angeles CA: Mötley Records/Beyond Music/BMG. (Originally released 1989, remastered 1999.)

Waters, R. (1975) Have a cigar [recorded by Pink Floyd]. On <u>Wish You Were Here</u> [compact disc]. New York, NY" EMI Recordings (Originally released in 1975, remastered in 1992, re-released in 1994).

Notes

i Motley Crue (1986). Although, as noted, this sentiment could have been uttered by any Metal Glam band between 1983 and 1992.

ii Both Maxx Factor and Marshall are name brands that serve to identify Metal Glam of the 1980s. While the brand name Maxx Factor refers to mascara, a cosmetic staple used by Metal Glam performers with a heavy hand, Marshall is the name brand of the most widely used amplifier. These amplifiers are stacked one upon the other to provide a louder sound, filling more sonic space. The spectacle of a veritable wall of Marshall stacks (used as a visual joke in a Spinal Tap video, replacing the Great Wall of China with a winding wall of Marshall stacks) has become synonymous with Heavy Metal as the sonic power becomes a trope for sexualized power. A display of sonic power became so important in Heavy Metal that Judas Priest used "flats", or "shells" of Marshalls to present the look of extreme amplification.

iii Metallica song title from debut album, *Kill 'Em All* (Metallica, 1983).

iv Guns N Roses song from *Appetite For Destruction* (Guns N Roses, 1987). Despite the sophomoric rhyme scheme of the lyrics, this was among the break-away hits for the band, both musically and cinematically as the video documented the Donnington Festival, not only putting Guns N Roses on the map with British Heavy Metal, but also promoted the band domestically as an international success.

v Line from This Is Spinal Tap (Guest et al. 1984), in which Tufnel and St. Hubbins explain, in racist and homophobic terms, that their music is neither racist nor homophobic.

vi As testament to the Speedmetal identity of Suicidal Tendencies, bassist Rob Trujillo has just replaced Jason Newstead in Metallica.

vii Title of Kiss' third album (Kiss, 1975a). Here the title was intended as ironic in that the members of the band, known for comic-book-meets-kabuki makeup and highly stylized stage costumes, were photographed in suit and tie dress. It was later revealed that even the suits used for the album cover had to be borrowed as no member of the band owned even a shirt that buttoned.

[viii] The song lyric from the 1964 hit "Satisfaction", "trying to make some girl" was not appreciated by the Ed Sullivan censors on the 10/25/64 airing, nor was the title for "Let's Spend the Night Together", which was suggested to be changed to "Let's Spend Some *Time* Together" on the 1/13/67 broadcast.

[ix] the line "your trick with fruit was really cute/I guess that's how you keep your pussy clean" (Jagger & Richard, 1973) was garbled beyond comprehension

[x] Lyric from Black Sabbath's "Black Sabbath" (Iommi, et. al, 1970), from *Black Sabbath* (Black Sabbath, 1970). Arguably the anthem of Heavy Metal itself, in contention only with Deep Purple's "Smoke On The Water".

[xi] Lyric from Black Sabbath's "War Pigs" (Iommi, et.al, 1970b). If "Black Sabbath" is the anthem, "War Pigs" is the rallying cry of Heavy Metal.

[xii] Lyric from Steppenwolf's "Born To Be Wild" (Mars, 1968), often cited as the formative and identifying lyric of Heavy Metal.

[xiii] Song title from Aerosmith's second album *Get Your Wings* (Aerosmith, 1974). Aerosmith in 1974 was considered to be in the category of "Hard Rock" which was, at the time, indistinguishable from the category of Heavy Metal until the New Wave of British Heavy Metal in the late 1970s, when Heavy Metal became conscious of its genre.

[xiv] Mötley Crüe 's Tommy Lee cites Kiss' Peter Criss as a direct influence and Marilyn Manson proudly reports owning a Kiss lunchbox as a child.

[xv] Song and album title of Judas Priest's *Hell Bent for Leather* Album (Judas Priest, 1979). This was the album in which Judas Priest changed their appearance to the leather and studs looks, setting the format for Heavy Metal attire for at least two decades to come.

[xvi] Note that London was not central to Heavy Metal, this will become important in the outsider appeal of the genre.

[xvii] Judas Priest is the exception, being a blues based rock band until their second album, and adopting the

traditional Heavy Metal leather studded garb by 1979's
Hell Bent for Leather album.

[xviii] This was also the time when the logo became essential for the Heavy Metal band. Prior to this point, band logos were few and far between. Kiss used one (actually, this was a significant part of the formation of the band (Kitts, 1994), Aerosmith's evolved by the fourth or fifth album (circa 1976, at the height of Kiss' popularity), and the Blue Öyster Cult had their identifying umlaut, but band logos were not widely used. Essentially, the logo is akin to a marketing device: it identifies the band as a product and tells the consumer something about that product. Weinstein (2000) notes that Heavy Metal logos have a sharp razorlike, electric or metallic appearance (consult the logos section of Appendix 2). This appearance connotes power, danger, and speed, qualities to be favorably compared to a Heavy Metal band. Following the NWOBHM it was rare for a band not to have a logo. In fact, Mötley Crüe notes that they met with label censure for changing their logo for each album (as cited liner notes, Mötley Crüe , 1991).

[xix] Lyric from Led Zeppelin's "Stairway to Heaven" (Page & Plant, 1971), the Heavy Metal classic from 1971 that simultaneously became a high school prom anthem and protest song, while also becoming background to countless Tolkein readings and Dungeon and Dragons duels.

[xx] An interesting juxtaposition is the band photo from Metallica's *Master of Puppets* album compared to the Mötley Crüe *Theatre of Pain* band photo. Both albums are the third for each band, both have the same year of release, both are West Coast bands, yet their visual presentation could not be any more different (see Appendix 2 for a comparison of the Mötley Crüe aesthetic and the Metallica aesthetic). While Mötley Crüe is poised and preened, coifed and costumed, Metallica are sprawled on a couch, clad in ripped denim, wearing Rock and Roll t-shirts, perhaps unshowered, and displaying divers dermatological abrasions. Speed or Thrash Metal denied the image and focused on the music.

Additionally, Speed or Thrash Metal, as the names suggest, interpreted Heavy Metal in an orthodoxy of loudness, speed, and intensity. The New Wave of British Heavy Metal's innovations in guitar technique and heaviness of drumming were heightened even more under Speed or Thrash Metal. Bands such as Metallica, Anthrax, Megadeth, Suicidal Tendencies, Exodus, Slayer, and Corrosion of Conformity, all West Coast area bands, took the Heavy Metal themes of power, oppression, the occult, and violence to new levels of intensity. Any wry humor that might have been displayed in Judas Priest and Iron Maiden was exorcised in Speed or Thrash

Metal to the result of a thoroughly humorless and
overly serious lyrical content and stage presence.

Also interesting to note is the intensity of the names of Speed or Thrash
Metal bands, a few of which have been cited above, are more extreme in violent
or dangerous imagery than either Metal Glam band names, or First or Second
Wave Heavy Metal band names.

While Metal Glam is considered to be the
outgrowth of the New Wave of British Heavy Metal and
British Glam, Speed or Thrash Metal is considered the
outgrowth of the New Wave of British Heavy Metal and
Punk. After American proto-punk of Iggy and the
Stooges, the New York Dolls, the Ramones, Television,
and Richard Hell and the Voidoids inspired the London
1975-1977 Punk scene, spawning the Clash, Sex Pistols,
X-Ray Specs, Generation X, Sham 69, the Exploited, and
the Anti-Nowhere League, America was in turn inspired
by London (McNeil & McCain, 1996; Lydon, 1994; Savage,
2001; Marcus, 1989). The Sex Pistols and Clash tours in
1977-78 exposed a new generation of musicians to the
raw immediacy of Punk Rock, known for its sloppiness,
sonic chaos, irreverent attitude, rebellion, and self-
destruction. The American response to the stripped-down
post-modern sped up 1950s style Rock and Roll was to
achieve the same results of the Sex Pistols and the
Clash, only faster and louder. This became Hardcore.
This was the style of the new face of American Punk,
bands like the Dead Kennedys, the Germs, Blag Flag,
Suicidal Tendencies, Minor Threat, and the Bad Brains.
Songs were shorter, faster, fewer chords were used,
lyrics were generally more politically inspired,
content had more to do with oppression and rebellion,
and the vocals were often incomprehensible.
Additionally, the rate of singing required to keep time
with the music, which rendered the vocals largely
incomprehensible, also made carefully crafted lyrics
expendable. Lyrics for Hardcore songs were closer to
stream of consciousness manifestoes of rebellion or
revolt.

Metallica, a band considered one of the founding proponents of Speed or
Thrash Metal, cite as their primary inlfuences Mötörhead and King Diamond of
the New Wave of British Heavy Metal (Judas Priest and Iron Maiden stylings can
be detected as well in Kirk Hammet's guitar riffs), as well as the Misfits, an
American Punk band whose catalog spans the stylistic and chronological range of

169

early New York City Ramonian Punk in their early singles "Static Age" and "TV Casualty" to American Hardcore in their final album *Earth A.D.* (as cited in liner notes, Misfits, 1997). In fact, Glenn Danzig of the Misfits would move on to a proto-Death Metal[xx] project Samhain, and a more clasical Black Sabbath-inspired Heavy Metal band *Danzig,* which would eventually evolve into an Electronica project.

The lines between genre blur within the history of Rock and Roll. For instance, Iggy Pop, of Iggy and the Stooges, is known as the "godfather of Punk" (Deane, 1995; McNeil & McCain, 1996; Marcus, 1989), yet Iggy is also associated with the British Glam movement in the 1970s. Some bands move from one genre style to another, such as the Misfits example above.

Another example is Suicidal Tendencies, whose first album was typical West Coast American Hardcore. The songs reflected adolescent marginalization and alienation, most poignantly displayed in the album's hit "Institutionalized" which recounts the narrative of an adolescent hospitalized by his parents, as well as political and social rebellion as illustrated on the albums songs "I Shot Reagan", "Two Sided Politics", "Subliminal" and "I Saw Your Mommy and Your Mommy's Dead". The photographs were of poor quality, and much of the album appeared to be produced by hand. These were all the hallmarks of Hardcore Punk. Within a year the band's follow-up was released. This album's graphics were much cleaner, their logo appeared more robust, and the album cover sported a muscular figure brandishing weapons, album's title: "Join The Army". From the first to the second album Suicidal Tendencies had gone from being a Hardcore band to being a Speedmetal band (see the Suicidal Tendencies album cover comparison in Appendix 2). Previously, the fan base for Punk had been entirely separate from that of Heavy Metal (Weinstein, 2000; Marcus, 1989; Hebdige, 1979; Savage, 2001).

The lines between one genre and another became more malleable during the 1980s. Part of this was the evolution of genre itself: Heavy Metal was establishing itself as a genre in the beginning of the 1980s as a result of the New Wave of British Heavy Metal, it consolidated by the mid 1980s allowing for genre subdivision between Metal Glam and Speed or Thrash Metal, and then the genre became diffuse again as Metal Glam faded and Grunge entered in the late 1980s/early 1990s. Heavy Metal's history is one of fusion with other forms of music, in the case of its inception, the fusion of blues-based Rock with psychedelia and post-Altamont biker culture. Rock and Roll itself is a hybrid of blues, folk, and elements of jazz improvisation. The fact that Speed or Thrash Metal results from a fusion of Heavy Metal and Punk provides an interesting counterpoint to Metal Glam's resulting from a fusion of Heavy Metal and 1970s British Glam.

[xxi] Song title from David Bowie's 1971 album *Hunky Dory* (Bowie, 1971) in which Bowie wears a dress on the

170

original version of the cover, changed for U.S. audiences. This was the album Bowie launched into Glam with, including the gender-bending anthems "Oh, You Pretty Things" and "Changes".

[xxii] Television and print media became more integral to music in the early 1970s, as the recording industry became more organized around marketing and selling to particular audiences. The mass popularity of Elvis, then the Beatles and Rolling Stones changed the recording industry to move with the change in consumer and to begin to keep up with and later anticipate these changes.

[xxiii] Line from "Sweet Head" (Bowie, 1974), an outtake from *The Rise and Fall of Ziggy Stardust and the Spiders From Mars*, which surfaced on the 1992 Rykodisc re-release of the Bowie album. A previously unreleased song, this could have been British Glam's rallying cry with its overt polymorphous sexuality and stylistic guitar riffs.

[xxiv] In the late 1960s/early 1970s the single was still the primary unit of consumption.

[xxv] The Tolkein inspiration is noteable in that Led Zeppelin began incorporating Tolkein themes as early as their second album's "Ramble On" (direct references to Mordor and Golem), which would become later embellished in their epoch-making fourth album known as "Zoso" or the "Runes" album.

[xxvi] It is interesting to note that this development was concomitant with Kiss' make-up design.

[xxvii] Marilyn Manson would reenact this during his stage show in the late 1990s.

[xxviii] Bowie would continue to push the envelope of Glam until 1975, when he reinvented himself again in a postmodern Christopher Isherwoodesque lounge incarnation before reinventing himself again in 1977 as a minimalist while he and Iggy Pop retired to Berlin to detox from heroin. As also will be seen in the track record of Mötley Crüe , the theme of an artist reinventing himself by both name and image, as well as reinventing himself through detox are recurrent throughout Metal Glam as well.

[xxix] Line from David Bowie's "Lady Stardust" (Bowie, 1974), a song about Lou Reed and the gender-bending Velvet Underground, made the subject of a film by XXXX *Velvet Goldmine*.

[xxx] Song title by Chinn/Chapman (1973), which became a runaway hit for the Sweet, later covered by Dokken.

[xxxi] Song title from Kiss' 1977 *Love Gun* (Kiss, 1977) album, written by Ace Frehley, Kiss' lead guitarist. This was the start of a pattern in which the groups' best songs were written by Frehley, to the frustration of band leaders Stanley and Simmons.

[xxxii] There is a suggestion that UK has been more accepting of "gender bending" than the USA, some of these reasons will be briefly touched upon in the Appendix.

[xxxiii] Song title from Motley Crue's 1983 album *Shout At The Devil* (Motley Crue, 1983). The Satanic overtones need little highlighting here.

[xxxiv] Punk Rock would follow Glam's lead in the Dickensian stage name for characters such as Darby Crash, Johnny Rotten, Sid Vicious, and Poly Styrene.

[xxxv] Song title from Motley Crue's album *Shout At The Devil* (Motley Crue, 1983), the video from which will be discussed herein.

[xxxvi] Bowie's *Diamond Dogs* was to be a concept album based around Orwell's 1984.

[xxxvii] The "13" was likely added for effect

[xxxviii] Song title by Lutz & Koda (1975), covered by Motley Crue on *Theatre of Pain*, the height of Metal Glam in 1985.

[xxxix] Song title from Motley Crue's first album, *Too Fast For Love* (Motley Crue, 1981), which to this day sound more Mott the Hoople and The Sweet influenced than their later riff-heavy Metal inspired works.

[xl] Album title fro Poison's debut album (Poison, 1986).

[xli] As mentioned above, Poison helped to solidify Metal Glam and pushed the Glam aspect further. They were an example of a "crossover" band that was able to attract a younger audience due to less objectionable content than Mötley Crüe or Ratt, and were able to attract a larger female fan base due to the aesthetics of the band. This, and the use of the music video as a vehicle to promote the band and especially the "look" of the band (and the visual packaging was to become a key point at this point in time, as exemplified by Poison), allowed the genre of Metal Glam to reach out to broader and wider audiences, and although in order to reach broader and wider audiences some aspects of the genre

of Heavy Metal had to be toned down (in the case of Poison, there is little violence in the lyrical content, although the misogyny remains intact, although to a lesser degree than in Mötley Crüe), they are still present, as will be seen in the next chapter.

[xlii] As Poison was seen as less threatening than other Metal Glam bands they were therefore more acceptable to parents, thereby garnering younger audiences, as well as a larger female fan base.

[xliii] Song title from Nirvana's 1991 *Nevermind* album (Nirvana, 1991), which blew the lid of Metal Glam and the music industry itself. The stadiums, clubs, guitars stores, and MTV were forever changed after the Grunge challenge to Glam.

[xliv] Title of Megadeth album, 1988, Capitol Records. Interesting side note: Megadeth lead guitarist Dave Mustane was in the original line up for Metallica.

[xlv] Mott the Hoople song title, [date of release]

[xlvi] Van Halen Song title, from Women and Children First

[xlvii] Acapella Rap group from the 1980s. This band also grappled with the meaning of masculinity and what it means to be a man in a positive urban light.

[xlviii] Jane's Addiction song title, Nothing's Shocking, This album was on the cusp of the transition from Metal Glam to Alternative. Jane's Addiction had the volume, the riffs, and the overdriven guitar sounds of Heavy Metal, but lead singer Perry Farrell (peripheral) may have been too gender bending in his long dreads, dramatic eye makeup and opera length gloves. He would mime fellatio on a microphone during their song "C'mon Ted, Just Admit It" (about Ted Bundy), the chorus of which is "sex is violent". This may have been too over the top for the current culture of Metal Glam when this album came out in 1988, but Janes Addiction set the pace for alternative bands to come like Nirvana, the Red Hot Chilli Peppers, and the Smashing Pumpkins. Also, I was hit on the head with a microphone stand by Perry while seated in the second row. They were opening for Iggy Pop.

[xlix] Kiss song title, Destroyer album, 1976, Casablanca records. Kiss, more than any other band, perhaps perfected the misogynist song lyric. Although their official anthem is "Rock and Roll All Nite" (and party

every day), a larger sampling of their song catalog
includes statutory rape ("Christine Sixteen"),
prostitution ("She", "Black Diamond", "Room Service",
"Ladies In Waiting"), and the various sexual triumphs
of the Rock and Roller ("King of Nighttime World",
"Great Expectations", "Firehouse", "Calling Dr. Love",
and "Love 'em and Leave 'em"). Masochism does not
enter the Kiss vocabulary as would be suggested by the
title of this song, whose chorus is "Sweet pain/my love
will drive you insane", suggesting that the pain is
given not received. The closed we come to masochism in
Kiss lyrics is guitarist Ace Freheley's breakaway hit
"Shock Me" with rhyming tag lines "make me feel
better", "put on your black leather" and "we can come
together". Sadly, this is the most sexually mature
sentiment expressed in Kiss' lyrics. Ace Freheley was
removed from the group four or five years after this
song.

[1] Reference to White Zombie's 1995 third album,
*Astrocreep: 2000 – Songs of Love, Destruction, and
Other Synthetic Delusions of the Electic Head*, this
album was effectively the last for White Zombie, who
had combined forms of Heavy Metal and Industrial, using
samples and tape loops. Due to extensive lawsuits which
significantly delayed the re-printing of their second
and most successful album, 1992's *La Sexorcisto*, lead
singer and founder Rob Zombie had to develop his own
samples rather than appropriate them from the archives
of cinema and television.

[ii] Guns N Roses song title, Use Your Illusion I, 1992,
Geffen Records. This song was one among many that
earned Guns N Roses the scorn and criticism of
feminists, recording authorities, and, well, people who
were offended at the misogynist message of the title.
Perhaps presaging controversy (or acknowledging it) Axl
is heard at the end of the song suggesting that the
song was a personal experience and not meant to have a
larger message. He would use that defense for most
criticism of the band's material. Other songs that
raised ire by Guns N Roses were: "Used to Love Her"
with the next line "But I had to kill her"; the
aforementioned "It's So Easy" [see Chapter One]; and
"One In A Million" with the line "Police and

174

niggers/get out of my way/I don't wanna buy any of
your/gold chains today".
[lii] Mötley Crüe song from the 1986 album of the same
name. This is an interesting turning point for Mötley
Crüe as Nikki Sixx describes the group shedding its
Glam image for a "street image" of jeans, leather
jackets, and motorcycles. The new "tough" look is
interesting as though it were backlash or compensation
for previous unmasculine behavior, especially in the
phallic imagery of the motorcycle. The setting of the
record cover photos taking place in a strip club, and
the title song having to do with objectification of
women appears to be further compensatory behavior.
[liii] The aspect of homoeroticism here should be
addressed, as it may be confusing given the
hypermasculine and heterosexist premise of Heavy Metal.
Walser (1993) makes several references to the
homosocial aspect of Heavy Metal and points out that
generally, when women are depicted in Heavy Metal
videos or lyrical content, they are either sexually
objectified or "the enemy". This leads to Walser's
statements of exscription of the feminine in Heavy
Metal. In almost entirely male genre, the images
connoting hypermasculinity, the tropes of power as
symbolized by cars, motorcycles, guns, bomber planes,
may also be read as homoerotic in the emphasis on the
phallus and ejaculatory explosion. Homosexual overtones
in song and album titles, such as Judas Priest's *Ram It
Down*, *Screaming for Vengence*, *I'm Your Turbo Lover*,
Aerosmith's *Rock and a Hard Place*, Accept's *Balls to
the Wall*, and Kiss' *Lick It Up*.
[liv] This is the first track off Mötley Crüe 's 1989 *Dr.
Feelgood* album. In this context, Tinseltown refers (as
well as in the Mötley Crüe context) to Hollywood,
particularly to the Sunset Strip, which was the
breeding ground for Metal Glam for at least a decade,
recently chronicled by Klosterman in Spin magazine,
September, 2002.

[lvi] Lyric from Led Zeppelin's "Stairway to Heaven" (Led
Zeppelin, 1971). The line goes "If there's a bustle in
your hedgerow/Don't be alarmed now/It's just a spring
clean for the May-Queen". This line has never made

sense to me, and it probably related more to Tolkein and neo-pagan imagery Jimmy Page and Robert Plant were into at the time. However, I use the line here to suggest an undercurrent, something moving beneath the surface that is troubling or disruptive to the previous order.

[lvii] Lyric from David Bowie's "Rebel, Rebel", (Bowie, 1974) from the *Diamond Dogs* album, among the icons of 1970s British Glam.

[lviii] Dialog from the 1984 film *This Is Spinal Tap* (Guest, et.al, 1984) in which the (fictional) band is visiting Elvis' gravesite to attempt putting their own longevity into perspective, and lead singer David St.Hubbins observes "Yeah, too much fucking perspective". Derek Smalls, bassist, rebukes him for his use of profanity in front of the King.

[lix] Song title from Skid Row's debut album (Skid Row, 1989).

[lx] Lyric from Pink Floyd's "Have a Cigar" (Waters, 1974), from *Wish You Were Here* (Pink Floyd, 1975). Although Pink Floyd has not been cited much in the body of this work, it should be noted that the bulk of Pink Floyd's classic period (from 1972's *Dark Side of the Moon* through 1979's *The Wall*) trades heavily in adolescent discontent and rebellion. The teenage *sturm und drang* coupled with a Sallingeresque angst-confusion makes Pink Floyd almost required listening.

[lxi] Lyric from Motley Crue's "Kickstart My Heart" (Sixx, 1989). The reference here is to Erikson's *stage* model.

[lxii] Not to be forgotten, the first stage, Basic Trust vs Basic Mistrust may be seen as instrumental in men's relationships with women, as highlighted by Faldui's illustration of the Spur Posse, the Citadel cadets, or the militia men who openly display distrust of women.

[lxiii] Lyric from Cheap Trick's "Surrender" (Neilsen, 1978). Cheap Trick is a hard band to fit into our genre categories: two of them were pretty enough to be Metal Glam, there was enough pop appear to fit into that genre, although chronologically, they were a bit too early for Metal Glam, with their first album surfacing in 1977, also making them too old for 1970s Glam. By the token of their pop appeal, they were just a shade too "light" to be categorized Heavy Metal, despite the

guitar virtuosity of Rick Neilsen. Cheap Trick serves as a less in Rock and Roll timing, that despite the songwriting talents and marketing of the band, they were ahead of their time and did not muster enough longevity to ride the wave of Metal Glam when their time finally did arrive. Cheap Trick will go down in the annals of Rock and Roll as a band people will scratch their heads over, wondering why they never "made it".

It should probably be mentioned that the focus of this lyrical reference was to Kiss records and the couch, awakening the allusion of the analytic couch.

[lxiv] Title of 1989 Ministry album. Ministry provides a link between Industrial and Heavy Metal with this album. Previously a synth-pop band aiming for club hits, Ministry took to metallic guitars and virtually invented a genre that combined loop percussive programming and sampling with an aggressive and powerful raw sound. It was this Ministry album that paved the way for Nine Inch Nails and Marilyn Manson, who would become the sound that replaced Heavy Metal in the 1990s, so influential that Motley Crue felt the need to move in the direction of the Industrial sound on their 1994 self titled album as well as their 1997 Generation Swine album.

[lxv] Song title from Monster Magnet's *God Says No* album (Monster Magnet, 2001). Monster Magnet represents a recent wave of Retro-Metal acts which draw heavily on the riffs and rhythms of the classic period of 1970s Heavy Metal. Monster Magnet lodges their sound firmly in Hawkwind's psychedelic jams while retaining science fiction and Satanic references nodding acknowledgement to Black Sabbath. Significant of the Hawkwind redux aspect of Monster Magnet is the fact that Lemmy Killmister, founding member of NWOBHM cornerstone Motorhead, was briefly Hawkwind's bassist. Additionally, Motorhead's theme song was originally recorded while Lemmy was still in Hawkwind.

[lxvi] Line from Mott the Hoople's Glam anthem "All the Young Dudes" (Bowie, 1972). Hoskyns (1998) cites the story of how Ian Hunter, lead singer for Mott was about to throw in the mascara and Bowie interceded, giving the band this song and hit record. Hoskyns (1998) also

177

recognizes that Mott the Hoople never really appeared to feel comfortable in their Glam identity, perhaps explaining why the remainder of Mott's recording career was closer in sound to a straightforward R&B influenced Rock and Roll than to the patented Bolan/Bowie sound of British Glam.
[lxvii] Speculated reasons for this include rising divorce rates, among other factors.
[lxviii] This is the sing-a-long chorus to "Cum On Feel The Noize" (Holder & Lea, 1973), originally a hit for British Glam's Slade, re-recorded for the new generation of Metal Glam audiences by Quiet Riot in 1983. The strength of Slade's song (and frequent MTV airing of the Quiet Riot video) was largely responsible for the success of Quiet Riot's *Metal Health* album. Hugely popular in 1983, sadly this was their high point as the band quickly disintegrated shortly thereafter.
[lxix] This is mere speculation, although student membership in APA as well as enrollment statistics in APA accredited graduate programs in psychology could be referred to in order to confirm these estimates.
[lxx] Title of Kiss' 1981 album *(Music from) The Elder*. This was Kiss' attempt at a high-concept album, desperately trying to recoup the success of their 1977-1979 extended 15 minutes of fame via ex-Alice Cooper and ex-Pink Floyd producer Bob Ezrin. *(Music from) The Elder* was without a doubt the worst album Kiss ever made, even die-hard fans, who buy the record only out loyalty yet never listen to it, despise it and credit the album with the further disintegration of the band. An important lesson is gleaned from the *Elder* incident, though: know yourself. Kiss had no business attempting a mytho-poeic sword-and-sorcery concept album, they were truly out of their element. Every band, however, needs to have at least one clunker album. The problem is that Kiss has had more than one.
[lxxi]   Somewhat like Jim Morrison, Carl Jung had to be dead for at least ten years before he made it big in America. Despite the fact that Jung was among the Psychoanalytic Landing Party of 1909, when Freud was invited by G. Stanley Hall to speak at Clark University, Worcester, Massachusetts, America has always hailed a more favorable reception to the Father of Psychoanalysis than to the Band of Brothers that would attempt an intellectual primal act (Freud as the Father of

178

Psychoanalysis, with his disciples, including Adler and Jung, who went on the 1909 voyage with Freud, as his "sons" that would, in Freud's eyes anyway, reenact the primal horde of brothers and kill and eat the father as described in *Totem and Taboo* - as cited in Freud, 1950/1913). Authors such as John Demos have speculated on why the United States were so fertile for Freudian foundations, but relatively little has been written on why Jung has only recently enjoyed a spotlight. Most every major U.S. city boasts a Jungian Institute, although they tend to be small operations that double as radical-intellectual bookshops (whose number may be dwindling with the growth of the internet and availability of obscure and radical psychological titles online). As space precludes entertaining *why* Jung was not mainlined into the psychological or intellectual culture of America until later, we are left with observation *that* the works of Jung made their way into the second half of the Twentieth Century, particularly beginning in the 1970s.

Publication histories of the larger publishing houses, such as Princeton University's Bollingen Foundation, Vintage and Viking presses document an increase in Jung's written works being re-published in the United States starting in the mid 1970s, and continuing to rise at present. As a quick example, the publishing history of *Psychiatric Studies*, hardly the juiciest of Jung's *oeuvre*, runs from its initial English translation in 1957, to a printing in 1970, 1975, 1978, and 1983 (Jung, 1983/1957). The significance of this publishing minutia is to illustrate that there was a *demand* for the works of Jung beginning in the 1970s.

[lxxii] Line from Lou Reed's "Make Up" (Reed, 1972), from the 1972 album *Transformer*. This was Lou's second solo album following the Velvet Underground, and among the important albums in the British Glam canon. Although Lou was Long Island born, and has come to be an iconic representation of New York City, at this point in his career he was identifying himself with British Glam. He wanted to be sent to London by his label, RCA, and have the album produced by up-and-coming Glamster David Bowie. Bowie, in turn, wanted to produce Lou's album to bring him closer to Andy Warhol and the New York City Factory scene. This reciprocal fascination between England and the United States traces back to the very birth of Rock and Roll and continues at present with the Strokes and the Vines emulating a British sound while European bands like the Hives and the

179

Hellacopters struggle to sound American. The inclusion of this Lou Reed line from the Transformer album will become an important point of foreshadowing in this work as our next chapter considers the differences between British Glam and American Metal Glam.

[lxxiii] Although it should be noted that Postmodern Feminist Theory has been finding footholds in curriculums of graduate Psychology programs.

[lxxiv] This line usually announces the repeated chorus at the end of a song. Although this is not limited to Heavy Metal or Metal Glam, Heavy Metal in general tends to be more "performative" than other forms of Rock and Roll. The sections of the songs are more likely to be announced, such as the intro with "C'mon!", guitar solos with "Guitar!" and drum solos with "Drums!". The postmodern aspect of Metal Glam as a recombination of Heavy Metal and British Glam leads to the transparent structure and theatrics, but we may also read these announcements as a celebration of the music form itself. Other genres may have lyric content describing discontent with Rock and Roll, but this is rare to find in Metal Glam.

[lxxv] I have seen this statement attributed to both Nietzsche as well as Dovstoevski.

[lxxvi] Clinical Psychology emerges out of the World Wars. An interesting exploration might be the examination of war alongside developments in psychology, as WWII helped Clinical Psychology emerge, the era of the Korean War carried with it a prominence in psychological assessment, dynamic theory, and behavioral theory, and Vietnam ushered in the Age of Trauma. A closer look might prove interesting.

[lxxvii] Song title from Ace Frehley's solo album (Casablanca, 1978), one of the four Kiss solo albums released simultaneously. Despite Ace's often marginalized role in the band, his solo album was the most critically acclaimed.

[lxxviii] Although Heavy Metal maintains a sense of history and tradition as back catalogs to Heavy Metal bands that have been defunct for years still sell, as other genres of Rock and Roll do not maintain such a strong sense of history.

[lxxix] Grand Funk Railroad song (Label, 19xx) that became an anthem for the Rock and Roll touring lifestyle.

[lxxx] Although the New York Dolls were often photographed in full drag, their behavior and antics never allowed their sexuality to be questioned.

[lxxxi] Inlcuding the line from "Street Hassle": "That cunt will never fuck again" (Reed, 1978)

[lxxxii] Johnny Thunders song from *Hurt Me* album (1985, Rose Records). Thunders was the lead guitarist for the New York Dolls as well as an icon for Punk guitarists.

[lxxxiii] Reference to Mötley Crüe's "God Bless the Children of the Beast" on *Shout At the Devil* (Mötley Crüe, 1983).

[lxxxiv] The mysteriousness of this song likely set a generation of adolescents to work with Ouija boards attempting to contact Morrison after his death, those who were not content with Ouija boards took to locating his grave at Pierre La Chase Cemetery, Paris, graffiting Oscar Wilde's grave along the way, and another faction of young Doors fans refused to believe Morrison was dead at all, but had been spotted locally and internationally with a slightly lessened frequency than Elvis, but higher than Marilyn Monroe.

[lxxxv] Rollingstone ran a cover story on Morrison with the title: "He's hot, he's sexy, he's dead" some ten years after Morrison's death.

[lxxxvi] This was reminiscent of the Punk movement of the late 1970s/early 1980s. These movements in Rock and Roll tend to move in polar fashion, going from the focus on stardom to the role of the "everyman" (or in the case of Lilith Fair, every*woman*). Note the shift from the Led Zeppelin/Kiss 1970s to the Sex Pistol/Clash 1970s, to the Mötley Crüe/Poison 1980s, to the Nirvana/Pearl Jam 1990s to the Kid Rock 1990s, and presently back to an everyman Eminem/Sum 41 model of Rock and Roll.

[lxxxvii] Not to mention the underlying assumption that women could be interchangeable as long as their hair color and body type was similar as noted in the transition of Suzanne Sommers to two other women playing the role.

181

[lxxxviii] "Unwashed and Somewhat Slightly Dazed", song title by David Bowie on the *Space Oddity* album (RCA, 1969).

[lxxxix] Song by Kiss (1974a) which signifies the end of their live show. Not only does this song represent the culmination of their musical themes in structure and arrangement (shared vocals, guitar solo and drum outtro) but this song conceptually represents Kiss' *raison d'etre*.

[xc] Kid Rock had his 15 minutes at the very end of the millennium, part of his image and attraction was his status of self proclaimed "Pimp of the Nation". An interesting side note is his current paramour, Pamela Anderson (ex-Lee). It should be noted that Ms. Anderson had previously been involved with Brett Michaels, lead singer of Poison, later to be married to Tommy Lee, of Mötley Crüe. As each icon fell in status their relationship with Ms. Anderson also disintegrated. Perhaps we could have taken a shortcut in this work and used Pamela Anderson as a barometer of hypermasculinity.

[xci] Eminem's fifteen minutes are concurrent with this writing. In terms of masculinity and popular culture, Mr. Mathers (aka Eminem) is infamous for misogynist lyrics directed toward his ex-wife as well as mother. Additionally, his lyric content could be argued to struggle with coming to terms with fatherhood and masculinity in the present era.

[xcii] The Donnas are a post-Punk/post-Glam band of four women, each adopting the moniker Donna a la the Ramones. In terms of Rock and Roll and Gender, the Donna's Runaways-redux act uses many standard Rock and Roll clichés about sexual exploits on the tour circuit, yet with young women singing these lyrics, gender roles become destabilized and attention is called to the fixed notions of gender and gender role.

[xciii] And again, the Judas Priest story is intriguing here, the one in which lead singer of the band that was most championed by homophobic Heavy Metal youth, announces his being gay.

[xciv] Lyric from Joan Baez' "Diamonds and Rust", covered by Judas Priest (Judas Priest, 1977, 1979b). Covering a folk song was an unusual move for Judas Priest,

although it should be kept in mind that when they released *Sin After Sin* 1977, they were not yet classified as Heavy Metal, this genre only became forged after *Hell Bent For Leather* (Judas Priest, 1979a).

[xcv] The "conflict" with Iraq at the time of this writing is reminiscent of the "conflict" with Iraq during the 1980s.

[xcvi] Title of 1985 Rainbow album. The significance of the group Rainbow lies in the fact that the group's founder and lead guitarist, Richie Blackmore, was one of the core members of Deep Purple, who penned the Heavy Metal anthem "Smoke on the Water" in 1972 and helped define the sound of Heavy Metal.

[xcvii] Title of Led Zeppelin's "posthumous" album, becoming one of the best selling albums of the early 1980s.

Made in the USA
San Bernardino, CA
10 July 2013